Buying & Selling Sports Collectibles on eBay®

Buying & Selling Sports Collectibles on eBay®

Bill Froloff

SVP, Thomson Course Technology PTR: Andy Shafran

Publisher: Stacy L. Hiquet

Senior Marketing Manager: Sarah O'Donnell

Marketing Manager: Heather Hurley

Manager of Editorial Services: Heather Talbot

Associate Acquisitions Editor: Megan Belanger

Senior Editor: Mark Garvey

Associate Marketing Managers: Kristin Eisenzopf and Sarah Dubois

Developmental Editor: Brian K. Proffitt

Project Editor: Kevin Sullivan, Argosy Publishing

Technical Reviewer: Chris Monahan

Thomson Course Technology PTR Market Coordinator: Elizabeth Furbish

Copy Editor: Tonya Cupp

Interior Layout Tech: Eric Rosenbloom

Cover Designer: Joel Sadagursky and Mike Tanamachi

Indexer: Larry Sweazy

Proofreader: Kim Cofer

ISBN: 1-59200-502-0

Library of Congress Catalog Card Number: 2004108013

Printed in the United States of America

04 05 06 07 08 BH 10 9 8 7 6 5 4 3 2 1

THOMSON

COURSE TECHNOLOGY

Professional ■ Trade ■ Reference

Thomson Course Technology PTR, a division of Thomson Course Technology
25 Thomson Place
Boston, MA 02210
http://www.courseptr.com

For my wife, Karen Froloff, and our children,
Alyssa, Alexander, and Christopher,
without whose remarkable love,
uplifting smiles, and undying support
this book would not have been possible.

Acknowledgments

It has been my lifelong dream to write a book, and thanks to the remarkable folks at Thomson Course Technology PTR, the dream has become reality. My most sincere thanks must go to my Acquisitions Editor, Megan Belanger, first for allowing me to pen this work, and then later for providing me with the unwavering support and superhuman patience that helped bring it all to fruition. From beginning to end, Megan's unique blend of poise, humor, and understanding helped keep my spirits up during the periods I needed it most.

Kudos also must go out to Project Editor Kevin Sullivan of Argosy Publishing. Kevin's wealth of knowledge in the publishing world and his easygoing attitude were invaluable to a writer who was finishing up his first book project. Thanks to his never-ending support and wonderful communication, we were able to incorporate the latest changes on eBay and keep the text up-to-date at the time of publication.

I would also be remiss to leave out the terrific contributions from Developmental Editor Brian K. Proffitt, Copy Editor Tonya Cupp, and Technical Reviewer Chris Monahan. The insight and input of these three wonderful people helped bridge many previously unrecognized gaps in several sections of this work. Their good work helped transform a rough first draft into what I believe is a comprehensive and informative final product. Compositor (or Layout Tech) Eric Rosenbloom, Proofreader Kim Cofer, and Indexer Larry Sweazy helped ensure that the look and content of the book pages kept those high standards. Here's hoping we all can collaborate on another project, and soon.

Finally, my heartfelt appreciation goes out to the thousands of friends I've made through eBay. It has been my privilege to interact with this wonderful community of online traders. Even if only a few of you benefit from reading this book, then I will have done my job. It is my sincere hope that I will continue to have the opportunity to interact with you, and to serve you, for many years to come.

About the Author

BILL FROLOFF is a businessman and writer who has bought and sold sports memorabilia for more than 40 years. His highly acclaimed business, 65 Mustang Sports, is based primarily on eBay, where he has earned recognition as one of the most knowledgeable and trustworthy PowerSellers of sports memorabilia in the eBay community. One of his most prized sales was a baseball signed by Babe Ruth and other members of the cast from *The Pride of the Yankees* (the 1942 film about the life of legendary New York Yankee Lou Gehrig). Inscribed "To Irving" and autographed by Walter Brennan and Gary Cooper along with "The Bambino" himself, the ball is believed to be a treasure once owned by composer Irving Berlin, making it a classic—just like the automobile for which the 65 Mustang Sports collectibles company is named.

A lifetime love for sports and a 30-year career in sports journalism paved the road for Bill's passionate venture into the world of online auctions in 1998, and he has never turned back. As a sportswriter, he covered everything from Major League Baseball's spring training to the Super Bowl and the NBA Championship. He also has authored several articles for such noted sports collectible publications as *Sports Collectors Digest,* and his hobby expertise has been quoted in publications such as the *Cincinnati Enquirer* and *Honolulu Advertiser.* He lives with his wife and three children and their cocker spaniel in Orange County, California, where he helps coach his sons' Little League teams in his spare time.

Contents at a Glance

Contents

Introduction

If you're a sports fan, you've probably bought some kind of sports memorabilia sometime in your life. Folks can buy all kinds of stuff at the ballpark or at the stadium, ranging from jerseys to hats to balls and photos. There are keychains, trading cards, blankets, bobble head dolls, and even cookbooks designed for fans who love their particular sport, who hold a specific team close to their hearts, or who want to show their pride for the alma mater.

Fans spend millions of dollars every year on these goodies. And because there is a market for cards and autographs and memorabilia, it comes as no surprise that Buying and Selling Sports Collectibles is one of the largest, fastest-growing, and most profitable categories associated with the wide, wonderful world of eBay. By just using your computer, you can buy or sell anything from a World Series ticket stub to a game-used jersey.

Need to buy a birthday present and don't have the time to shop? Odds are, you can find the perfect item to buy on eBay.

Cleaning out a closet and come across a set of old football cards you no longer want? What better place to sell them than on eBay?

Have a set of Olympic pins that came as a birthday present years ago, and would rather have a baseball signed by a current major leaguer? Why not sell the pins on eBay, then use the funds you receive to buy the autographed baseball?

The wonderful thing about online auctions and eBay is that you never have to leave the safety and comfort of your home or office to participate. People don't care how you look or how you speak, and you don't have to be related to the Rockefellers (at least distantly) and be formally invited to some fancy-schmancy auction house in the heart of Manhattan.

The auction house is *your* house, or your workplace, or anywhere you can log onto a computer and type "www.ebay.com" into your browser. It's quick. It's simple. It's easy. And it puts regular, hard-working folks on equal footing with millionaires. How wonderfully American is that? A computer doesn't care how much money you have in your bank account, but using that same computer to buy or sell goods online can help you put more money into your savings account or retirement fund.

So, plug in your computer, open your Internet browser, and get ready for what could be the most fun game you've ever played in your life—the buying and selling game associated with eBay.

Pregame Stretch

You very well might earn enough money, after reading this book and implementing its knowledge, to surpass even your wildest dreams. But the primary goal here isn't to help you get rich quick. I won't promise you a vacation home in the Caribbean, but this book will help guide you over some of the rough spots if you want to buy and sell sports memorabilia on eBay. Information contained within is guaranteed to help you avoid some of the pitfalls that will come looking for you as you begin, or try to perfect, your online trading experience. Those same pitfalls were the ones I personally experienced to a certain degree, and the ones I want to help you sidestep.

Developing a Game Plan

If you are just starting out on eBay, this book is for you. But there also are entire sections pertaining to the buyer or seller who is looking for new ways to grow their collection or develop their business. Pick out the section or sections that appeal to you, and you'll be sure to learn something new.

The online auction phenomenon has taken root in our lives and in our communities. While eBay once was just a tiny seedling that sprouted out of the imagination of Pierre Omidyar, it now has grown into a towering, sinewy oak tree, constantly branching out in new directions every year. This book was written for those folks who are searching for a way to climb aboard, but it also contains information that can prove valuable for those people who are already a part of the ever-expanding eBay family tree and aim to climb even higher.

Now it's time to get ready to play.

Here's the Lineup

Each chapter of this book is designed to help you deal with different hurdles that a collector or seller must clear if he is going to be successful on eBay. These include:

Chapter 1   Sports Collectibles and eBay: A Marriage Made in Heaven

■ Why sports collectibles and eBay are a perfect match.

■ How the advent of online auctions spelled doom for some owners of the quintessential baseball card shops that once were a collector's main conduit to the hobby.

Chapter 2   Pledge Allegiance to eBay

■ How to register on eBay, with instructions taking you step by step through this process.

■ How to sign up with PayPal, generally recognized as the preferred payment vehicle for a majority of eBay auctions.

Chapter 3   Do Your Homework Before You Buy

■ How to search for an item on eBay.

■ How to determine how much to pay for an item once you find it.

■ Why some folks collect trading cards while others prefer autographs and memorabilia.

Chapter 4   Authentication Is Sweeping the Nation

■ Why it's now in vogue for collectors to authenticate their sports collectibles.

■ How the FBI got involved in the hobby.

■ Tips on figuring out who you can trust, or not trust, in the vast eBay marketplace.

Chapter 5   Getting Ready to Bid

- How to bid on an eBay item.

- Why feedback ratings are important.

- How to keep tabs on your bids.

- How much to bid and when to bid.

- How to complete your purchase after you win an auction.

Chapter 6   Getting Ready to Sell

- How to sell better by designing a tempting auction format.

- Why quality photos are important to promote sales.

- How descriptions, timing, and other details are important to a prospective customer.

Chapter 7   The Auction Process

- Why it's important to cross-merchandise your auctions.

- How to build an eBay store.

Chapter 8   Closing the Deal

- How to close the deal after you've made a sale.

- Why it's important to ship securely.

- How to deal with buyers who don't pay up.

- Why you should learn to communicate with your customers.

Chapter 9   Next Steps

- Ways to expand your business with easy-to-use tools available right on eBay.

- Why earning PowerSeller status can boost your sales.

The Opening Pitch

OK then, the stage is set. The buyers are ready. The sellers are ready. An online audience of millions is prepared to watch the proceedings via computer, and perhaps even take part. You can feel the tension in the air . . .

Ready to play ball, eBay-style?

part 1

Warming Up

chapter 1

Sports Collectibles and eBay: A Marriage Made in Heaven

It all began with me trying to track down Mickey Mantle. Maybe you have a similar story from your own childhood?

When I was in fifth grade, my younger brother and I pretty much ate, slept, talked, or played baseball all day, every day, all year long. We were dedicated baseball fans and fervently followed all the Major Leaguers, worshipped the guys in The Show, even envied all the raw-talent rookies with peach-fuzz chins and unshakable dreams of making it in the Big Leagues. We emulated their batting or pitching styles in our backyards or the local diamond.

Like many other youngsters our age, baseball was on our list of required studies. And boy, did we do our homework! We could recite by heart almost every player's batting average and home-run totals, where they were born, their hobbies, and in what year their rookie cards were printed. We were such fans, we'd squirrel away all the pennies, nickels, and dimes we could get our hands on, until we'd saved enough to bicycle down to the corner market and trade in our change for a few factory-fresh packs of baseball cards. Remember how *good* they smelled?

Okay, so it *was* that tiny slab of bubble gum that gave those cards that familiar, comforting smell. But that aroma was only part of our fascination, and a small part at that. Often we'd shove the gum aside so we could get on to more important matters—those cards!

We'd wildly tear open the packs and sometimes sort them out right there on the sidewalk, not even waiting to get home. We were hoping to find the face of some star player—*any* star player—on those fabulous little pieces of cardboard. There were five cards in a pack back then, and I would always dream the day would come when I could shout out to nobody in particular, "Hey, I got the Mick!" It was my sincerest hope that after sifting through my packs that I could proclaim myself the proud new owner of a baseball card bearing the name, face, and statistics of New York Yankees legendary slugger and eventual Hall of Famer Mickey Mantle. As you might have guessed by now, it wasn't to be. But it never stopped me from trying! Most times I had to settle instead for somebody like Bob Uecker: "Great cards, eh, buddy?"

So why do we collect?

We didn't open those packs of cards just to put them in the spokes of our bicycle tires (even though that's where a lot of them later wound up). Collecting cards or autographs or other forms of sports memorabilia was great fun. It's one that can develop into a healthy passion. We all learn at a young age that society admires its highest achievers, and we strive to model ourselves after them. Along those lines, professional athletes are lifted onto a pedestal and placed in a spotlight that makes them nearly impossible to overlook. We see them every day on television and we read about them in the newspaper. Our favorite television shows are even preempted by professional baseball, football, or basketball. Ask my wife to share her thoughts about that last one. On second thought, better not!

We're inundated with so much information about athletes that we may think we know them personally and call them by their first names. "Hey, did you see that shot Kobe made last night?" someone might ask by the water cooler. You know right away he isn't referring to the chef at the local Japanese steakhouse. To bring these current-day fables even further into our lives, many fans (remember, fans is short for fanatics) also show their allegiance by buying cards, photos, or autographed balls. They spend millions of dollars every year collecting.

It should be noted, of course, that some segments of the collecting population also look at buying cards or autographs as an investment. The hobby can become a sports fan's own personal version of Wall Street, with collectors buying or selling items featuring whichever athlete is hot at that particular moment. (Let it be said that I believe there's nothing wrong with a collector hoping to profit over time from the purchase of a particular collectible, even though the purist might beg to differ.)

Honestly, isn't that why many collectors search out that coveted rookie card? Don't fans crowd around baseball stadium dugouts before games and flock near player exits after games, just hoping to get an autograph? Maybe they can't afford to buy it on eBay. Isn't getting it in person more fun anyway? And don't some of them figure they might be able to sell it on eBay to help pay for that vacation in Hawaii? Often we'll read stories in newspapers or magazines about collectors who struck it rich by "cashing in" a collection they built up and saved for years or even decades. So what's the difference between that and selling something for profit a few days, weeks, or months after first purchasing it? Not much.

And this is where eBay (www.eBay.com) comes in. This giant web site offers everything from A to Z, and sports memorabilia is a large part of that. Hundreds and thousands of transactions between buyers and sellers take place every day, with sales ranging from a 50-cent common card to a one-of-a-kind game-used jersey that might cost tens of thousands of dollars. That is what makes eBay the perfect place for a sports collector—you can shop all day and browse though thousands of items without leaving home! And when you do decide to make a purchase or a sale, the postman or the UPS driver will make sure your item is delivered right to the front door of its new owner.

Caution: Collecting Can Become Infectious

Once you get started collecting, it's not always easy to stop. Sports memorabilia in the United States dates as far back as the late 1800s, when tobacco companies printed collectible cards featuring baseball players and professional boxers. By the 1920s, it was every baseball fan's dream to get Babe Ruth's autograph on a baseball. Those dreams are alive today; for many baseball collectors, locating a hard-to-find T-206 baseball card, or one of those vintage autographed baseballs signed by "The Bambino," can rank as the silver chalice of one's collection.

Our classic memories remain, but my brother and I are 40-plus years older. Some of our friends might kid about keeping some oxygen handy should we try to ride our bikes down to that same corner market today. We both still love to eat, sleep, and talk baseball; now I do so with my own kids, who are burgeoning baseball fans and collectors in their own right. Just as those carefree bike rides to buy baseball cards are history, so too are many of the baseball card shops that once previously flourished.

Where Did All Those Baseball Card Shops Go?

Today a multitude of companies sell dozens of types of cards. Cards are produced for baseball, basketball, football, hockey, soccer, and tennis. Then there are several prominent memorabilia companies that sell only balls, jerseys, and photos that have been personally autographed by well-known sports figures.

Note

Autographed memorabilia pairs with the issue of cost. Companies obviously pay big bucks to have a contracted athlete sign for them, so their items aren't cheap—and then there's the ever-expanding field of autograph authentication, which I address in Chapter 4, "Authentication Is Sweeping the Nation." Be sure to study these sections if you plan to buy or sell autographs on eBay, as forgeries abound in this area, and there are several useful ways to determine whether an item is real or a fake. Nobody wants to waste their hard-earned cash, so this is an important section to study and understand.

Thirty years ago, nearly every little town had its own baseball card shop. It was usually just around the corner; perhaps your city had two or three. After all, collecting baseball cards, or any sports memorabilia for that matter, has long been a part of Americana. While the demand for sports collectibles continues to go up, the number of baseball card shops has declined markedly. A simple look in the phone book will prove it.

Used to be, you could plan your Saturday afternoons around a trip down to the local card dealer. He would always have the latest news on the newest cards. Boxes and boxes of unopened wax packs would be stacked behind the counter. The supplies were on the other end of the store—the plastic nine-card sleeves in which to store your valuable commodities. (You didn't want the corner of that Darryl Strawberry rookie card getting bent, did you?)

The shop owner was almost a member of the family—a distant uncle, you could almost say. "Uncle Bob" knew you by your first name, was in tune with your likes and dislikes, was aware that you were trying to complete a set of 1956 Topps baseball cards, and knew how much money you wanted to spend. It was fun; it was easy; it was familiar; and it was a simple way to continue your collecting pursuits.

The changing economy wasn't friendly to many card shop owners, who found themselves battling higher rent, higher overhead, and lower sales. For card shop owners, things worsened to the extent that their profit margins either shrank considerably or withered up and died altogether. About this time they also faced a baseball card explosion of sorts, as card manufacturers decided to expand their production lines. Instead of the regular Topps, Fleer, or Upper Deck offerings, each card company opted to develop new card series, each company trying to outdo the next. Then along came the jersey cards (with pieces of game-used jersey in them) and autograph cards (signed by the star players everyone wanted to collect).

The baseball card market bulged to the point of oversaturation. How was poor old Uncle Bob supposed to know what cards to carry? Too much of a good thing was not a good thing. Uncle Bob didn't know what to do. Like many card store owners, unable to pay the bills, he had a going-out-of-business sale and closed up shop.

You can also blame it on the Internet. More precisely, you can blame it—at least a lot of it—on eBay. eBay's size and scope continues soaring higher than a Barry Bonds tape-measure home run in San Francisco. At the same time the number of sports memorabilia stores has declined. The fact is, the phenomenon of lost baseball card shops can partially be traced back to the advent of eBay. Many card store owners have been forced to close up shop over the past few years, with many likely realizing that a battle with eBay was a war they couldn't win. And for good reason.

An estimated two-thirds of Internet users in the United States (about 83 million people) have joined the ranks of online shoppers, according to the *Pew Internet and American Life Project*. *Pew* director Lee Rainie said data about online shopping collected by Pew shows "growing e-commerce activity" as the number of Internet users continues to grow, too. Rainie called that trend important "because it's a bigger slice of a bigger pie." Statistics on gender and ethnicity of online shoppers mirror those of people who go to retail stores.

According to eBay's own figures, it has more than 104 million registered and confirmed users worldwide, buying and selling everything from sports cars to time shares to game-used jerseys and autographed baseballs. Those same figures also show eBay has 12 sales categories that each top $1 billion in annual sales, including the Sports category at a whopping $2 billion in estimated sales every year all by itself. In the first quarter of 2004 alone, this e-commerce giant reported a record $8 billion in gross merchandise sales, while also reporting that its annual earnings had nearly doubled over the previous year to $200 million. If you own a small card shop, how can you compete with that?

As an individual collector, isn't it time for you to make sure you get your fair share?

Join the Auction Crowd

Some folks probably thought eBay's founders were nuts, but just like the little acorn whisked off the tree by a strong gust of wind, that little nut has grown vigorously. There's no sign the massive Internet oak is going to come toppling down anytime soon. Sports fans like statistics, right? Here's some background on eBay, much like the back of those cards I love so much.

Note

Guess what? It's now in vogue to be a computer geek. I'm proud to say I'm one of them. And if you want to join the club, or maybe just become a bit geekier than you already are, this book offers some valuable lessons and helpful hints to move you in the right direction. We have some tried-and-true practices that should pay off whether you are a buyer, a seller, or both.

Pierre Omidyar's baby is recognized as a pioneer of online auctions, having begun an efficient person-to-person format that lets buyers and sellers decide the value of their items. Omidyar, a 1988 Tufts graduate, now serves as chairman of the board and full-time philanthropist. Founded in September 1995, eBay prides itself as being "The World's Online Marketplace" and is widely accepted as the most popular shopping destination on the Internet. On an average day, buyers and sellers from all parts of the globe converge to conduct business. Are you searching for a 10-cent card to complete a set? A $10,000 baseball signed by Babe Ruth? Rest assured you can pretty much find it on eBay. On any given day, millions of items across thousands of categories are for sale on eBay, enabling you to trade on a local, national, and international basis.

People spend more time on eBay than any other online site, making it the most popular shopping destination on the Internet. On an average day, millions of items are listed there. Here are just some of the categories:

- Art
- Books
- Cars
- Clothing
- Coins
- Crafts
- Electronics
- Home furnishings
- Pottery
- Real estate
- Stamps
- Tickets

Members from all over the world buy and sell on eBay. Currently, eBay has local sites that serve these locations: Australia, Austria, Belgium, Canada, France, Germany, Ireland, Italy, Korea, the Netherlands, New Zealand, Singapore, Spain, Sweden, Switzerland, Taiwan, and the United Kingdom.

The site has a wide variety of features and services that enable members to buy and sell quickly and conveniently. Buyers have the option to purchase items in auction-style format or at fixed price through a feature called Buy It Now. In addition, items at fixed prices are also available on Half.com, an eBay company. Some of the site's services include these beauties:

- Online payments by PayPal
- Wide array of Buyer and Seller tools
- Developers Program for community members who want to develop their own solutions

Note

As of December 31, 2003, eBay had over 5,000 employees. eBay now is run by Meg Whitman, who as president and CEO of the company was ranked by *Fortune* magazine as the third most powerful woman in business in 2002. This company must be doing something right!

Save Money, Save Time, Save Your Sanity

Here's the deal: Why hop into your SUV, fill the car with gasoline, battle the freeways, get to the overcrowded shopping mall, and then fight with the weekend spenders for a parking space?

Instead, park yourself in front of your computer and log on to eBay; you're in business. Collectors can decide online if they want to shop exclusively in their nearby locale, in any of the 50 states, or anywhere in the entire world, for that matter—all with just a simple click of the mouse. Still searching for that Wilt Chamberlain rookie card? Just click the Search button, type in your search criteria, and *voilà!*—a dozen choices may pop up for your consideration. All this without having to leave the comfort and safety of your home or office.

Make no mistake: The savvy baseball card shop owners have learned to incorporate eBay into their business model. Those sellers likely continue to thrive as much as before eBay (or perhaps more). It's not unusual to walk into your local neighborhood card shop (if you have one!) and spot the owner seated next to one of his display cases, busily typing up eBay auction listings, sending off email invoices, or monitoring his day's online sales. Other sellers, on the other hand, have converted completely from physical storefronts to exclusive e-commerce stores and are loving it. Less overhead means bigger profits.

Hopefully by now, you can see that mastering better ways to buy and sell sports collectibles on eBay is in your best interest—*and* your pocketbook's. Even if you use just one of many suggestions in the chapters to follow, you should save more than enough money in the long run to pay for this book. Isn't saving or making money the whole idea here?

It is the wise eBay buyer and seller who studies history and learns from it. It was baseball immortal Satchel Paige who once said, "Don't look back—somethin' might be gaining on you." This wise Hall of Fame pitcher's words ring so true for buyers and sellers alike when it comes to dealing with sports collectibles.

All Aboard the eBay Express

Since its birth nearly 10 years ago, buyers and sellers have had to get on board, or get steamrolled over, by this runaway locomotive known as eBay.

I'll be honest: Some collectors still swear on making hands-on, face-to-face purchases only, and there exist some quality card shops and sports memorabilia shows for those who decide that is the way they want to go. Many collectors prefer the instant gratification of handing their money to another live person and being able to touch, examine, feel a new item that they hope to add to their collection. For many of these folks, eBay may not be their favorite option. But let's be clear about this, too: The buyer or seller who disregards eBay altogether is doing himself, his business, his hobby, and his collection a terrible disservice.

Be aware that this book isn't public relations for eBay; like most eBay users, I have suffered the web site's ups and downs since becoming a member in 1998. I can still remember the days when, before improved hardware was built into the site, buyers and sellers didn't know when they would actually be able to buy and sell. The site would crash, and if you had a particularly expensive item you were interested in, well, tough luck. Today's version of eBay operates more like a Cadillac compared to the Model-T version of its earlier days. Six years of buying and selling on eBay also have helped me learn ways to avoid "deadbeats" whose main goal is to muck up business. There are several helpful hints in later chapters filled with tips on avoiding this mess.

It's my goal to help you avoid some of the painful pitfalls that I experienced and to help you learn from my own exhaustive late-night hours spent staring at my computer screen, studying my own online auctions and everybody else's! Never fear, the information is here. I guarantee that what you want or need to know is easier to find (and use) than that elusive Mickey Mantle card that I never came across!

Now it's time to take off the gloves, roll up your sleeves, get down in the trenches, and all those other tried-and-true clichés that routinely spill out of the mouth of athletes. It's time to get to work. Of course, if you're an eBay veteran looking to improve your skills, it might be best to skip past the next couple of chapters and get right to the meat and potatoes, beginning with Chapter 4. The upcoming appetizers were cooked up with the eBay novice and mid-level users in mind.

chapter 2

Pledge Allegiance to eBay

You must register as a member if you want to use eBay. This requirement protects both the buyer and seller and facilitates the completion of a transaction. Anybody can browse the millions of items up for bid, but only registered members can buy or sell them. After you get registered (and you must be 18 years old to do so), then you can get to the fun stuff. The registration process is free and easy, extremely user-friendly and even the most novice computer user will find that, after a few clicks of the mouse, the bidding process will become easily familiar. Be prepared to furnish some sensitive personal information that is not available to other buyers and sellers, only to in-house eBay folks who are sworn to secrecy! It's time to become part of the family. If you follow the next few steps, you will become a member of the club and can start taking advantage of those bargains!

Signing Up on eBay

It's now time to open the door to "The World's Online Marketplace." Once you gain admittance, buying or selling can become as fun and easy as breaking open a fresh pack of 1989 Upper Deck baseball cards. If you have not yet registered as an eBay user, this is Step #1. If you already are registered, you can go ahead and skip past this brief introduction.

Registering is free and painless, consisting of three easy steps. For users just getting started, your first step is the most important.

1. Find the eBay home page at http://www.ebay.com. You can see the page in Figure 2.1.

Note

Be prepared to furnish some sensitive personal information. The info isn't available to other buyers and sellers—only to in-house eBay folks who are sworn to secrecy.

The registration process consists of three easy steps. For buyers and sellers just getting started, your first step is the most important. You'll need to find the eBay home page at http://pages.ebay.com/index.html (shown in Figure 2.1).

2. It's now time to open the door to "The World's Online Marketplace." Once you gain admittance, buying or selling on eBay can become as fun and easy as breaking open a fresh pack of 1989 Upper Deck base-

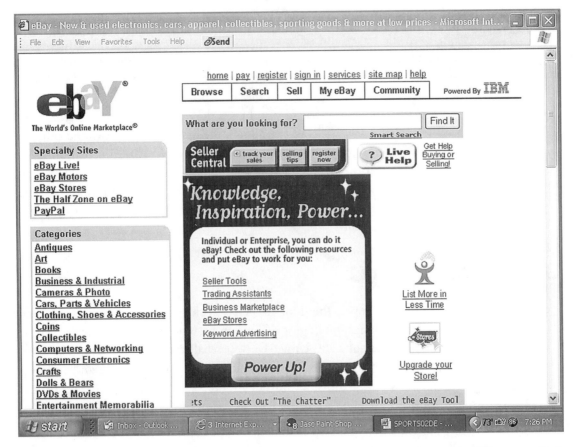

Figure 2.1

Click the Register tab on the top of the eBay home page.

ball cards. If you have not yet registered as an eBay user, this is Step #1. If you already are registered, you can go ahead and skip past this brief introduction. Click Register (at the top of the home page). You are directed to a page that looks like the one in Figure 2.2.

3. Enter your personal information. About this personal stuff: You need to input all the required personal information before you can join the buying and selling community. Rest assured that your personal data is stored in eBay's secure database. Once you are signed up you will feel a big relief, almost like the day after you get your income tax done every April. This is what's asked of you:

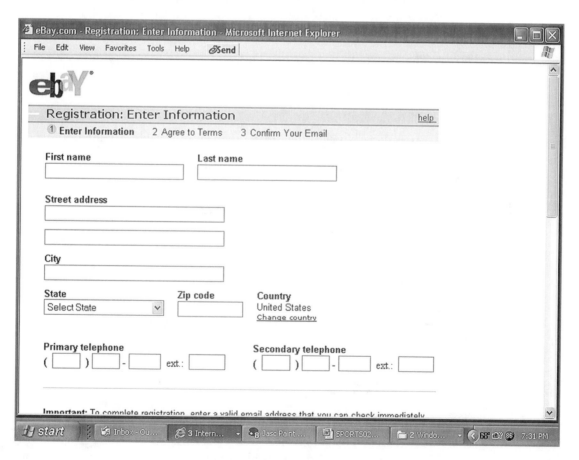

Figure 2.2

This is where you enter personal information needed to register on eBay.

- **Name.** Hopefully you know that.

- **Address.** And this.

- **Phone number(s).** Home, cell, or work will do.

- **Valid email address.** Your choice of email accounts is important because this is where you receive correspondence from eBay when you place a bid, win an auction, or sell an item. It's also where you receive information regarding registration confirmation.

- **User ID.** You have to choose one; this is how other users will know you. A good bet is to choose an ID that says something about you. For instance, if you collect autographed photos, you might want to become known as photoman. You can change your eBay ID later. eBay won't let you use your email address as your user ID.

- **The answer to a question.** This is for retrieval purposes in case you forget your password. There are several questions offered, and you should choose the one to which it's unlikely anybody but you would know the answer.

- **Birth date.** No cheating. eBay doesn't care if you're a Baby Boomer.

- **Credit card number.** You can use your Visa, MasterCard, American Express, or debit card here to pay for your eBay fees.

4. Once you have completed all the fields on this page, click Continue. The screen in Figure 2.3 shows up.

Continue registering through the next section. Rest assured, your personal data is stored in eBay's secure database. It might seem like you're signing your life away, but don't fret, you are almost there! Once you are signed up you will feel a big relief, almost like the day after you get your income tax done every April.

Terms of Agreement

You need to understand and agree to the Terms of the eBay User Agreement and Privacy Policy. The eBay police will make sure you are using the web site correctly later on and will quote details from the user agreement should you run afoul of the law. It's a legal document that spells out the relationship

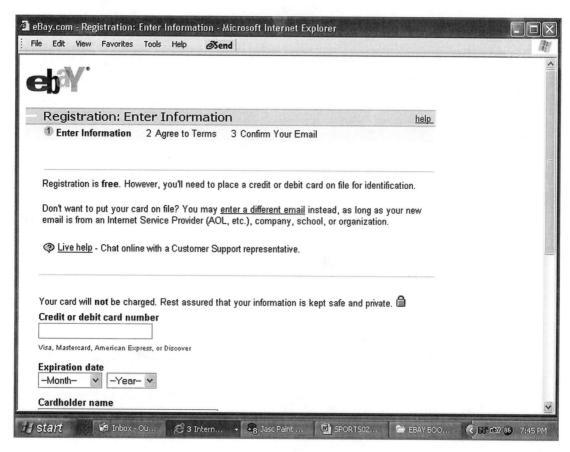

between you and eBay. This is a formality these days for using any secure web site. The terms eBay sets are established to protect and serve its community.

5. Read the Terms of the eBay User Agreement and Privacy Policy.

6. Select the box verifying you are at least 18 years old (if you are, that is).

7. Select the box confirming that you recognize that you can choose *not* to receive communication from eBay once you have completed registration. Some people (and they are in the minority) might prefer not to receive any email notifications from eBay at all, but who wouldn't want email from eBay if you were thinking of buying or selling on the site!

By selecting this box, you're telling eBay that it's okay for them to notify you via email that you've bid, been outbid, won an item, listed an item for sale, and so on. This is critical for keeping you informed. Once you agree to these terms, you are almost finished with the registration process.

If you want to complete the steps now and read the user agreement information later, skip to this chapter's "The Home Stretch" section.

Note

eBay reserves the right to amend its user agreement at any time by posting the amended terms on the site. Periodically, they do change. All amended terms are effective 30 days after they are first posted on the site, and you also receive notification of these changes in emails sent by eBay.

If you're under the age of 18, you can use eBay only in conjunction with, and under the supervision of, your parents or guardians. eBay also prohibits the transfer or sale of your eBay account (including feedback) and user ID to anyone else. If you are registering as a business, you represent that you have the authority to bind the entity to the agreement—in other words, you agree that you are officially designated by your company as having the authority to enter into a selling agreement by using eBay.

Fees and Caveat Emptor

Joining eBay is free, but fees are involved in some instances. Bidding on items is free, but eBay charges for listing sale items. You can review those charges before agreeing to begin an auction. You're responsible for paying all fees associated with using the site, and all applicable taxes, too.

While eBay is an auction marketplace, its user agreement points out the fact that it's not a traditional auctioneer. The site sees itself as a venue that allows anyone to offer, sell, or buy just about anything, at anytime, from anywhere, in a wide variety of pricing formats. eBay states plainly it is "not involved in the actual transaction between buyers and sellers" and says that it's not party to any disputes between buyer and seller.

There has been plenty of controversy about this last point, but eBay has successfully defended its position in some high-visibility lawsuits, maintaining it has no control over the quality, safety, or legality of the items advertised, the truth or accuracy of the listings, the ability of sellers to sell items, or the ability of buyers to pay for items. This also means eBay does not control an item's final price nor does it have access to the actual goods being sold and therefore cannot verify authenticity.

Covering Their Behind

Indeed, eBay covers its backside carefully. Witness this part of the user agreement:

> Because we are a venue, in the event that you have a dispute with one or more users, you release eBay (and our officers, directors, agents, subsidiaries, joint ventures and employees) from claims, demands and damages (actual and consequential) of every kind and nature, known and unknown, suspected and unsuspected, disclosed and undisclosed, arising out of or in any way connected with such disputes. If you are a California resident, you waive California Civil Code §1542, which says: "A general release does not extend to claims which the creditor does not know or suspect to exist in his favor at the time of executing the release, which if known by him must have materially affected his settlement with the debtor."

Now you know why lawyers and attorneys make so much money!

Much of the rest is pretty straightforward. If you're a bidder, you agree that your bid is a binding contract and that you'll complete the transaction with the seller and agree to the conditions of sale included in the item's description. It explains that bids are not retractable except in exceptional circumstances, such as these:

- The seller materially changes the item's description after you bid.
- A clear typographical error is made.
- You cannot authenticate the seller's identity.

If you choose to bid on mature audience items or items that are restricted to adult use, you are certifying that you have the legal right to purchase such items.

If you're a seller, you agree that you are legally able to sell the item you list and that your item is accurately described and pictured in the auction listing and in the proper category for sale. You also are obligated to sell the item to the highest bidder unless the buyer fails to meet the terms of your listing or you can't authenticate the buyer's identity. You can be suspended or have your account terminated should eBay suspect you have engaged in fraudulent activity on the site. Your item can be removed for sale if it infringes on the copyright or trademark rights of third parties. You also cannot *shill bid* (bid on your own items to artificially boost selling price); this is an infringement punishable by suspension from eBay.

You also can be suspended if eBay can't verify your account information or you earn a net feedback rating of –4. (Beginning with Chapter 5, "Getting Ready to Bid," we help you learn how to use the feedback tool to determine which buyers or sellers you can trust to do business with.)

The Personal Stuff

The personal information you provide is protected vigorously and the user agreement outlines this. They promise not to sell or rent your personal information to third parties for marketing purposes without your explicit consent, stating:

> We view protection of users' privacy as a very important community principle. We understand clearly that you and your information is one of our most important assets. We store and process your information on computers located in the United States that are protected by physical as well as technological security devices. We use third parties to verify and certify our privacy principles . . . If you object to your Information being transferred or used in this way please do not use our services.

The Home Stretch

You've completed the personal info and read the user agreement. Next comes the process of confirming your email address. After agreeing to the aforementioned terms, the next eBay screen asks you to check the email address you registered. If you've done everything right, you should have received an email from eBay (delivered almost immediately upon completing the first two steps). You need to read this email to confirm and then complete your registration.

8. Open the confirmation email (eBay's registration notice).

9. Click directly on the provided link to receive the news you've been waiting for. You can see that news in Figure 2.4 and Figure 2.5.

Congratulations! You are an official, non-card-carrying member of eBay, ready to match wits with the other 40 million people who buy things from this site.

If you want to start selling right away, continue with steps in the following section.

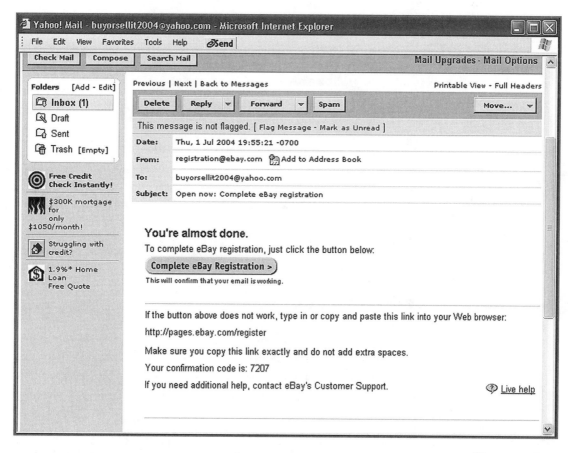

Figure 2.4

Click the link in the registration email to complete your account setup.

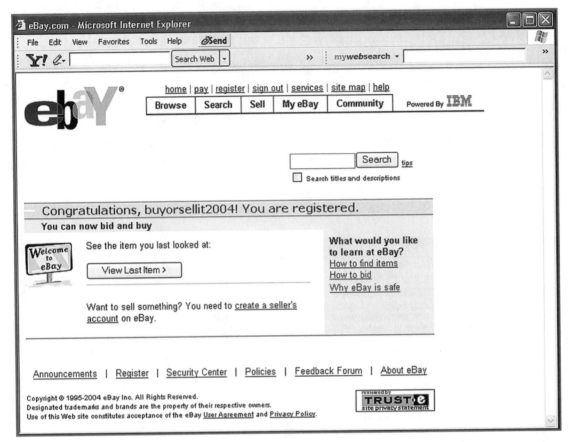

Figure 2.5

The good news is that you're now a member of the eBay community!

Setting Up a Seller's Account

At this point, you might be thinking you only want to use eBay to buy sports collectibles. That's fine. Rest assured, however, many a collector had that same thought and then decided that she really didn't need that Ken Griffey, Jr. rookie card. What better place to sell that card than on eBay?

The screen that appears after you complete registration directs you to the seller's market, so why not take a minute right now to get going? Have your checking account number and either a credit or debit card handy before beginning these steps. You need these to verify your information. The other option is to pay a $5 fee to use ID Verify, which confirms you are whom you say you are.

Remember, these steps (including credit card information) are built into eBay to protect you, to protect other eBay users, and to protect eBay itself. If these steps make you hesitate, that's understandable. You can always register as a seller later on, but for the sake of continuity, I address this issue right here and now.

10. Click the Create Seller's Account link. You're directed to the screen in Figure 2.6.

11. Enter your credit card or debit card number (see Figure 2.7) and click Continue.

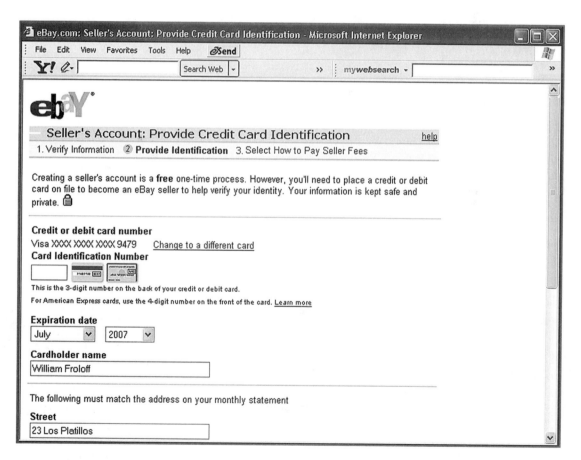

Figure 2.6

Fill out more information here to sell on eBay.

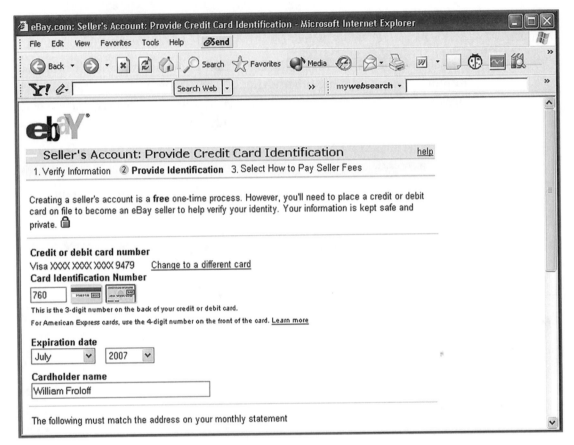

Figure 2.7

Here's where you take the first steps to selling merchandise on eBay.

12. You are asked to provide banking information, including these things shown in Figure 2.8:

- **Bank name**

- **Bank routing number**

- **Checking account number**

13. Click Continue.

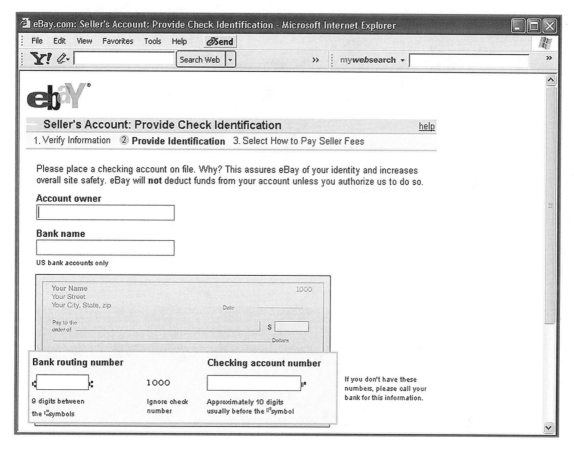

Figure 2.8

Have your checking account information handy to complete your seller's account registration.

14. Choose whether you want your seller fees deducted from your checking account or charged to your on-file credit or debit card. You can see this screen in Figure 2.9.

15. Click Continue and your account information is verified using encrypted data transfer. Once that is complete, you see a new eBay screen directing you to list your item for sale.

Before you start selling, though, put on the brakes and park your fast-moving eBay machine along the curb. I want to tackle another aspect that can help streamline your experience.

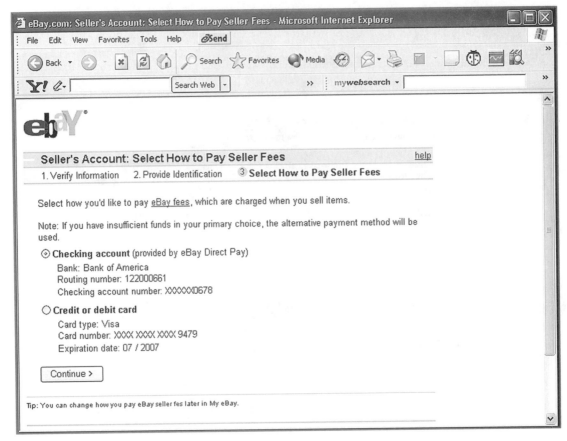

Figure 2.9

You have a choice of having your seller's fees deducted from your checking account or charged to a credit/debit card.

The Wide, Wonderful World of PayPal

Lots of buyers and sellers prefer using checks, cash, or money orders to pay for auctions. However, the quickest and easiest way I've found to transfer funds (other than by paying directly by credit card) is by using PayPal. Sellers can list PayPal, which is linked directly to the eBay site, as a payment options when they list an auction; buyers can search for items whose sellers accept PayPal.

Simply put, PayPal (www.paypal.com) is an electronic method of paying or receiving payment. You can send money to your seller or accept money from your buyer. It's so user-friendly that perhaps 95 percent of the people who purchase my items use PayPal to pay for them—honestly! It has built-in safeguards that protect your privacy, not to mention your credit card or bank account numbers. Your information is stored only in encrypted form on computers unconnected to the Internet. PayPal also professes that it does these things to protect you:

- Restricts access to your personally identifiable information to employees who need to know that information to provide products or services to you

- Tests security systems regularly

- Contracts with outside companies to audit security systems and processes

Note

PayPal's growth and popularity have spread like wildfire in recent years. The idea has worked so well, in fact, that eBay phased out its own payment company (Billpoint) and bought PayPal in October 2002. According to www.paypal.com, the system "enables any individual or business with an email address to securely, easily and quickly send and receive payments online. PayPal's service builds on the existing financial infrastructure of bank accounts and credit cards and utilizes the world's most advanced proprietary fraud prevention systems to create a safe, global, real-time payment solution." PayPal is a global player when it comes to online payments, claiming to have 40 million account members spreading across 38 countries.

My personal experience? A large majority of eBay buyers and sellers prefer using PayPal to complete transactions. The web site is committed to handling your customer information with high standards of security. Your credit card and bank account information are stored only in encrypted form on computers that are not connected to the Internet. PayPal also professes it restricts access to your personally identifiable information to employees who need to know that information in order to provide products or services to you, and that it tests security systems regularly and contracts with outside companies to audit security systems and processes. Plus, it's a time-saver. You can pay for, or get paid for, an auction literally seconds after the bidding is completed.

Please note that no system is perfect. Still, if you already access your bank account information online, using PayPal is not much of a stretch.

Many eBay sellers who accept PayPal also accept direct payment by credit cards (Visa, MasterCard, American Express, Discover) or allow you to pay by check or money order. Terms for completing a sale are listed within each auction. You're free to choose what item to bid on, when you want to bid, how much to bid, and how to pay for your item within the seller's parameters. Be prepared to wait a bit longer for the delivery of your item, however, if you pay by personal check. Many sellers hold off shipping merchandise for one to two weeks for items paid this way in order to avoid a mess should a buyer's personal check

Figure 2.10

Click Sign Up to begin PayPal registration.

bounce. PayPal, credit cards, and money orders generally are preferred by sellers and result in your much-anticipated package arriving quicker at your doorstep.

1. If you're ready to join the growing PayPal club, it's time to click Sign Up; see Figure 2.10 for what to expect.

2. You are directed to a screen that asks whether you want to create a personal or business account and in what country.

3. Furnish information similar to that when you signed up for eBay. You can see the screen in Figure 2.11.

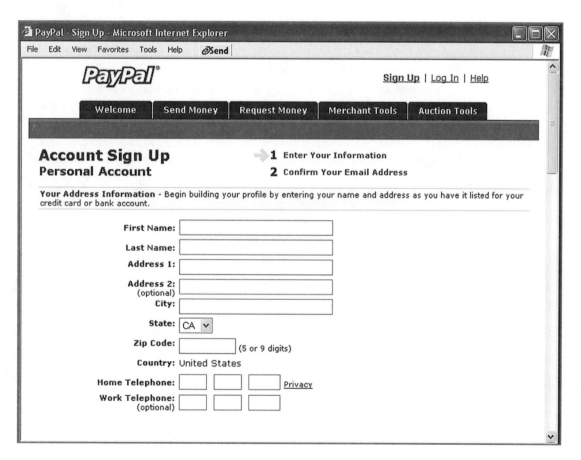

Figure 2.11

Be prepared to enter more personal information when you register for PayPal.

- **Name**
- **Address**
- **Phone number**
- **Valid email address**
- **Security questions (that you select and answer)**

4. Decide if you want your account to be a Premier account. You can leave this for later if you want by clicking No.

5. The PayPal user agreement and privacy policy appears. Read this information thoroughly so you understand your rights and privileges.

6. If you do agree to the terms, click Yes on both boxes and then click Continue.

7. Go to the email address you have registered under. You will have received a confirmation notice from PayPal like that in Figure 2.12.

8. Click the link within that email to confirm your registration (see Figure 2.13).

9. When you click the link to activate your account, you're prompted to provide the password you chose when you signed up with PayPal (see Figure 2.14). Type in your password and click Confirm.

10. Click My Account, which is shown in Figure 2.15. You now have access to PayPal and its services (see Figure 2.16). Nose around the web site a while. PayPal is pretty self-explanatory; it offers several links if you have questions.

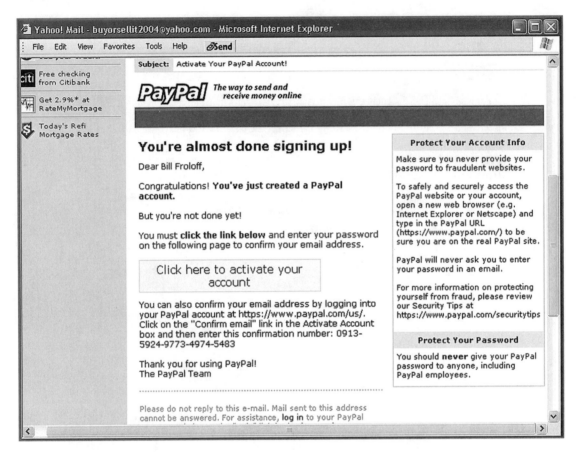

Figure 2.13

You can click on the link to activate your account.

Figure 2.14

Provide the password you chose when you signed up.

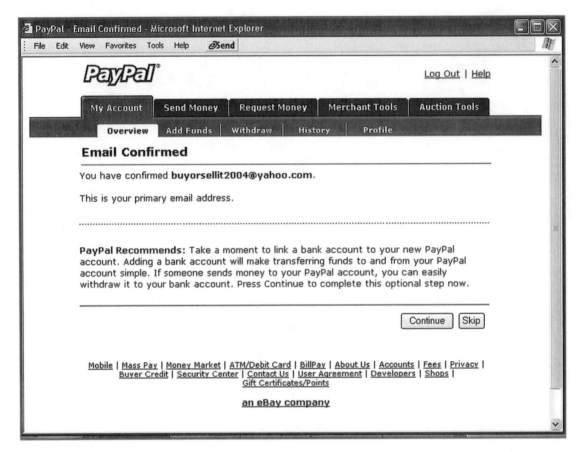

Figure 2.15

Click My Account and check out some of the web site's features.

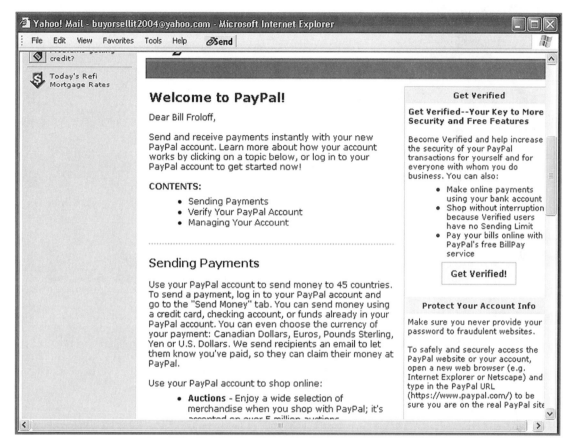

Figure 2.16

You're a registered member of PayPal!

Congratulations, you are almost ready to go! There's still some homework to be finished, however. But if you're ready to buy or sell, the next chapter starts you on the road to success.

part 2

Buying Sports Collectibles
on eBay

chapter 3

Do Your Homework Before You Buy

You've signed up with eBay and PayPal and you're raring to go, right? You're ready to buy? Prepared to spend that hard-earned paycheck? Locate that longed-for rare addition to your collection? Time out. You need to learn how to maneuver through eBay. Though the anticipation of that first shopping trip might have your fingers itching for clicking, your first step should be to master the Search function. You have millions of items to choose from, so becoming familiar with the tools you will use is of the utmost importance.

Doing so is nearly as simple as calling 411 to get a phone number. In this case, siphoning off the Mark McGwire rookie cards from the Mark McGwire autographed baseballs only takes a few seconds and a couple clicks.

How to Search for Your Item

You can find the search bar at the top of any page on eBay. On the home page you're kindly prompted by "What are you looking for?" Get ready to see the goods.

1. Click Search. The basic search mechanism appears, as shown in Figure 3.1.

2. Type your information into the Search Keywords or Item Number text box. The drop-down list next to this text box has options that can refine your search. They're discussed in further detail after these steps.

3. Click Search. A list of all the items on eBay with those words appears.

Notice that you may define your Search with the drop-down menu (All of these words, Any of these words, Exact phrase) so as to help narrow your search.

Refine your search with these options:

- **All of these words**
- **Any of these words**
- **Exact phrase**

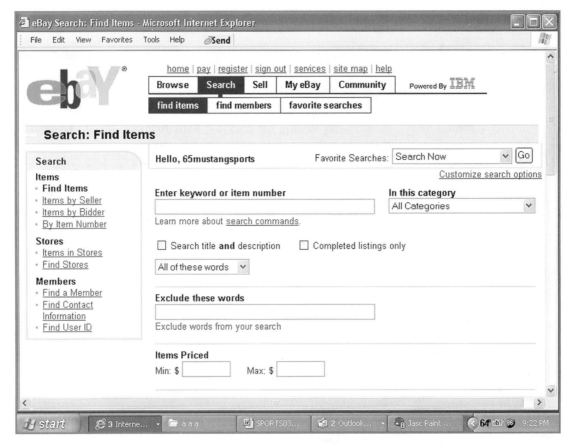

Figure 3.1

This is the first place to look when searching for an item on eBay.

Narrow the Field

Say you type in the words *Larry Bird Autograph*. You might come up with 100-plus different matches. To help narrow your search even further, check out the Matching Categories listing down the left side of the page. You get to see which categories include items that contain titles with the words you entered. Therefore, you might see an item listed under Autographs-Original, Memorabilia, Cards, or Other Sports Memorabilia. This breakdown makes your search job that much easier.

Now assume you are looking only for autographed cards. If you click Cards, you're directed only to the listings posted in this category—eBay sifts out the autographed 8 x 10 photos, which you may not be looking for. The exact opposite is true, too: If you're looking only for photos that Larry Bird autographed, then you'd click Autographs-Original, shown in Figure 3.2. You could also choose Cards or Fan Shop, which would lead you to different types of items. Table 3.1 breaks down these choices and lists examples.

Table 3.1 What You Click Is What You Get

Click This Category	You Wind Up Here	Example Item
Autographs-Original	Signed photos, signed jerseys, signed basketballs, and the like. Cards and unsigned items should not appear here.	A Boston Celtics jersey autographed by Larry Bird.
Cards	Cards, but could include autographed items from one of the major card companies. Any signed jerseys or signed photos should not appear here.	A card offered by a seller who has a trading card signed by Larry Bird.
Fan Shop	Memorabilia associated with a specific sports team.	In this instance, Larry Bird items would likely be included among the Boston Celtics Fan Shop.

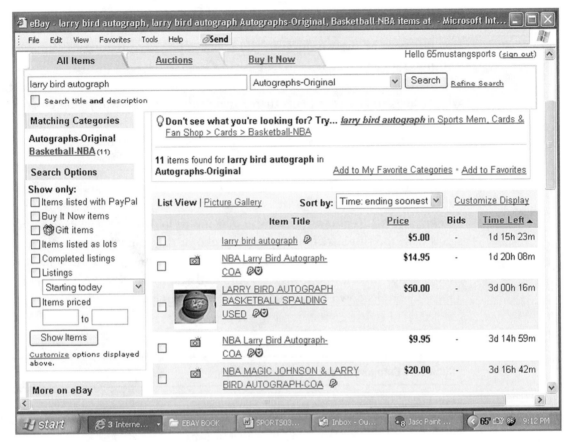

Figure 3.2

You can choose between Memorabilia and Cards when using the eBay search function.

Some items can fall into two or more categories. For instance, Autographs-Original may have the same item listed by another seller under Other Sports Memorabilia.

Another helpful section, called Search Options, appears below Matching Categories. Click the box to the left of any category and you can further refine your search for an item. Let's say you want to search only for items that include the Buy It Now option and are posted only by sellers who offer PayPal as a payment option. Click each of those boxes—Buy It Now and PayPal—and then click Show Items. The refined search list comes up on your computer.

By placing a checkmark in the box associated with each category, you can sort your eBay search to find sellers who have:

- Listed with PayPal as a payment option. They may offer other options in addition to PayPal.

- Buy It Now items. Things listed with an immediate purchase price and not necessarily falling under the classic auction definition, sold to the highest bidder.

- Gift items. A gift box icon promotes these items as good gift ideas, and a seller pays an additional fee to have this icon displayed next to their item.

- Lots. Lots are multiple items sold all at once, in bulk. They are usually like items (such as baseball cards).

- Completed listings. This options displays items that were sold over the past 30 days.

- Items that fall into a prescribed price range.

If eBay asks you to "sign in" again any time during your search, don't be worried. This is done as a precautionary measure to ensure only eBay registered users can use some site functions. You may be asked to sign in several times as you maneuver throughout the site.

eBay Stores shows up below the search options and includes items you are searching for. If you're looking for a Larry Bird autograph and are a lifelong fan, click one of those storefronts to see if that seller lists more Celtics items. Sellers who have eBay stores also put more time and muscle into selling on eBay, and therefore likely have a stronger feedback rating than some others (more on feedback later). An eBay store will include all of a seller's items, including store listings that have a "Buy It Now" price and do not actually meet the criteria of an auction item (which is sold instead to the highest bidder).

Go back to the eBay search page. (To get back to the basic Search page from a store—or from anywhere on eBay—just click on the Search button at the top of the page.) In addition to searching for certain keywords or by item number (each eBay auction listing is assigned a unique listing number), you have other choices, available by clicking on the link to More Search Options. These choices include:

- Words you wish to exclude from a search

- Price range you are willing to pay

- Items only listed in the Gallery view. Sellers can provide an image of their item for the Gallery view during the listing process, and the Gallery view allows shoppers to browse through auctions that only include these images. It's a nice way to visualize your purchase instead of having to click on every text listing just to see what the item looks like.

- Category in which you know your item is

- Region of the country

- Auction's end or begin date

- Highest and/or lowest price

Mastering the search function, of course, is the easiest way to finding those bargains everybody talks about where eBay is concerned. If you know a certain item's going rate and no outside market conditions are affecting its value, then locating that item at a reduced price is always enjoyable! That's the beauty of eBay.

Alert

If you're a buyer, consider either making sure your seller is a full-time dealer who sells items in brand-new condition or ensuring the item you're bidding on is not—and beware of this—a "recycled collectible." If the seller has displayed the item improperly, or has handled an item whose value can decline if it is not in mint condition, then you might be in danger of overpaying for this "recycled" item. Since the value of collectibles often hinges on condition, you don't want to spend any of your hard-earned cash on something that is damaged or missing its Certificate of Authenticity (a written guarantee that the item you are purchasing is authentic). This is not to say that every recycled item is damaged, but you can never be too sure. If you're uncertain, ask a seller how he obtained the item and in what condition the item is. If he balks at your questions, it's probably best to steer away from those items.

Searching By Seller

So you already bought an item or two on eBay from a particular seller and enjoyed the customer service associated with your purchase. The search engine lets you search for items being auctioned off by that seller.

1. Click the search page.

2. Click By Seller.

3. Type in the seller's name.

Let's use 65mustangsports as an example. If you have purchased from this seller before, then in your personal feedback profile, or in your list of previous winning bids on eBay, you would be able to find the seller's name associated with those previous purchases. If you have identified 65mustangpsorts in this case, then all the items being sold on eBay by 65mustangsports come into view if you click on the search page and define your auction search (see Figure 3.3) by Seller's Name. The resulting default view shows every item listed by a seller. At the top of that page, you can click on Auctions, which will show you *only* auctions listed by that seller, weeding out items listed in their eBay store. A Buy It Now tab is available if you would like to view the items that seller has for immediate purchase.

Supply and Demand

A word of caution about the completed listings discussed in the "Narrow the Field" section: Many buyers have lost out on an item they desperately wanted because they vowed only to bid up to the highest price that a similar item has sold for over the past 30 days. "That item sold for $20 just last week, so I am not going to pay any more than that today." The occasional fallacy is that market conditions can change drastically and in no time at all. When a player reaches a historical career milestone, is traded, or dies, it is not uncommon to see a sudden rush to buy items associated with that athlete. That can boost the price of those items. The lesson to be learned is that like everything else in a free market, supply and demand rules. If an item's for sale and few buyers want it, the prices most assuredly go down. However, if circumstances change, you'll probably encounter a mad dash to own a particular signed photograph, card, or football. You guessed it: The prices go up, up, up!

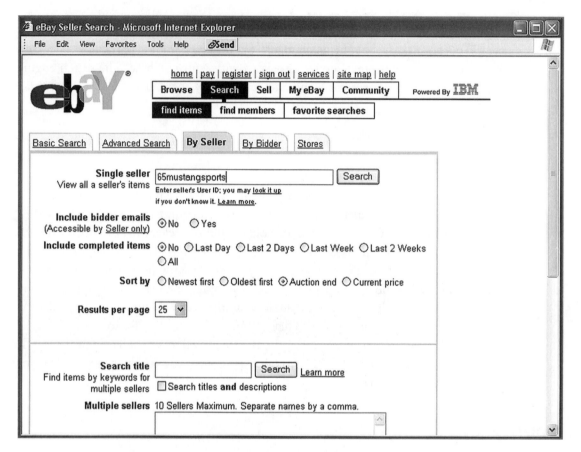

Figure 3.3

Click the By Seller tab to browse through a particular seller's auctions.

Here's a perfect example: Hall of Fame quarterback Johnny Unitas often made the autograph show rounds and the cost of his autograph—especially considering his record passing career, 10 Pro Bowl appearances, 3 NFL championships, and 1 Super Bowl triumph with the Baltimore Colts—was often extremely reasonable, perhaps in the $45 range. On September 11, 2002, a healthy-looking Unitas was working out at a physical therapy center when he suffered a fatal heart attack at age 69. The selling price of Johnny Unitas autographed 8×10 photos on eBay nearly tripled almost immediately. The stampede for Johnny Unitas items was on, and the selling prices reflected as much.

The bottom line: An eBay item is worth whatever a buyer is willing to pay for it on any given day.

Of course, several factors can influence the value of a sports collectible. For instance, if a baseball star hits three home runs in one game, his rookie card or autographed photo could double the very next day. The same holds true if a football team's star running back is enjoying a stellar season on a team that looks like a sure bet for the Super Bowl. The value of his items may increase gradually as the season progresses, reaching a crescendo if his team actually makes the Super Bowl or he smashes a long-standing record such as the NFL single-season rushing mark. Of course, the opposite can be true as well; if he is injured during the season, his team is unexpectedly knocked out of the play-offs, or he runs afoul of the law, the market value of his collectibles can shrink substantially.

Another factor that can drive up interest or prices on collectibles: Once an athlete is deemed worthy for election to the Hall of Fame, or just prior to his induction into the shrine, it's typical that the value of his collectibles will rise, too. That said, there generally is also a "cooling off" period soon thereafter, perhaps ascribed to the theory of "out of sight, out of mind." But when the Hall calls—or when Heaven calls—buying and selling prices tend to jump.

About 10 years ago, the 1989 Upper Deck rookie card for Ken Griffey, Jr. was valued at $100 or more. Collectors clamored for this expensive piece of cardboard and paid big bucks for one or more of them. They were then safely tucked away in card holders or professionally graded by one of the major card grading companies, whose thick plastic holders helped protect their investment. Griffey, Jr. made a huge splash when he first came up to the Big Leagues, hitting prodigious home runs in bunches. He also became the youngest player ever to hit 350 homers (28 years, 308 days), 400 homers (30 years, 141 days), and 450 homers (31 years, 261 days).

But Griffey, Jr. grew tired of playing in Seattle and swapped his Mariners jersey for a Cincinnati Reds jersey as part of a four-player blockbuster trade before the 2000 season. What followed was unfortunate, not only for Griffey, Jr., but also for the thousands of collectors who had invested huge amounts of money in his memorabilia. A series of injuries robbed Griffey of much of his playing time, and his rookie card value plummeted from $100 to $50 faster than you could say "grand slam."

There will be another chapter in the Ken Griffey, Jr. story. After regaining his health, he joined the 500 Home Run Club during the 2004 season. Sports fans everywhere again began speculating: Could this be the guy who eventually breaks Hank Aaron's all-time record of 755 home runs? This speculation likely will continue as long as Griffey, Jr. remains healthy and hitting home runs at a plentiful pace. The market value of his rookie card and other memorabilia undoubtedly will rise and fall with his accomplishments on the field.

Several collectors have perfected playing the eBay game. Some have meticulously done their homework, know the market conditions, noted current values, and scouted out an item they want to buy. If they have won an item at a fantastic savings, it is not unusual for them to turn around and resell that item later. Some experts go ahead and resell the item immediately, hoping for instant profit. Others, however, might hold onto a specific item for a time—until the athlete is splashed across the sports page or his team wins a championship.

This is why most collectors and dealers alike will always advise you to collect what you enjoy. Then, if the value goes up or down, you still have what you like.

What Is an Item Worth?

A lot by potential buyers ask me this question. They know I know the answer because my second home is eBay. (Although my wife might tell you it's my first home!) I do lots and lots and lots of research all the time. But the lesson to be learned here is simple:

Do your homework.

If you haven't done your homework, don't complain after buying something that you paid too much.

If you are in the market for a Mickey Mantle rookie card and thinking of buying it on eBay, check out the market. By using the Search page, you can see what items are currently listed for sale, who's selling them, what their selling feedback reputation is (see Chapter 4, "Authentication Is Sweeping the Nation"), what the item's condition is, and more. You wouldn't go out and buy a new home without checking around for the best deal first, right? So why not do the same thing if you are investing?

Another must-do for any savvy collector is checking out past sales.

1. Click on Search.

2. Type in words associated with the item you want to buy.

3. Before clicking Search, click the box that says Completed Items only. You can see it in Figure 3.4.

From there, you can sort the results by List or by Picture Gallery view, whichever you prefer. If you click List View, items appear in list form with only a description. If you click Picture Gallery view, items appear with a Gallery

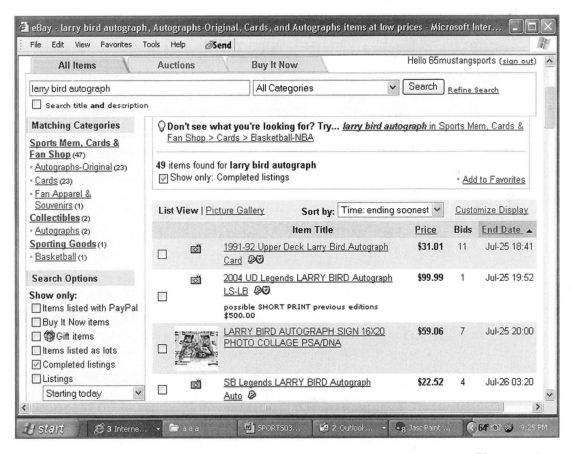

Figure 3.4

The completed listings search page helps you find out how much a similar item has sold for previously.

photo. Which one to use? This is a matter of personal preference, as some folks prefer an advance look at an item before clicking the actual listing. Other bidders find the thumbnail cumbersome and difficult to manipulate, particularly if they're using a dial-up connection that requires much more time to load the page.

More Reference Material

The eBay search mechanism shows you items that are (or were) for sale on eBay. You can use other methods to see how much an item is worth.

Several good weekly and monthly publications help collectors keep a pulse on the hobby. Beckett publishes monthly magazines for baseball, football, basketball, hockey, and other sports. Those magazines list the most current market values for sports cards and autographs. *Sports Collectors Digest* and *Tuff Stuff* magazines, shown in Figure 3.5, can be useful in this regard. In addition to price guides and stories about players, collectors, or collectibles, these publications obviously also include paid advertisements from many nationally known dealers. These ads can help educate a potential buyer. Check out books besides this one that deal specifically with sports collectibles and the items you hope to add to your treasure chest.

Publications also are useful for keeping tabs on upcoming sports card and autograph shows. Most bigger sports collectible shows either advertise the event or are included in a publication. These shows typically include appearances by several autograph guests; the ad includes fees for having items signed. That is often a good barometer of what the current market will bear. It is also from these public signings that many future eBay items emanate.

Even if you don't find what you're looking for at a show, it's a good idea to circulate with others who share your passion. You might get some useful advice from a dealer or fellow collector; that can translate into savings (or spending a few more bucks when necessary, as the case may be). Talk to dealers, interact with fellow collectors, ask questions and listen to answers. Study how sellers display their products. Again:

Do your homework!!

Figure 3.5

Tuff Stuff and *Sports Collectors Digest* are musts if you plan to buy and sell on eBay.

You might be through with high school or college, but the homework continues. I still have that occasional dream about not studying enough before a big test in college, causing me to toss and turn. I'm always relieved to wake up and realize, "Hey, that was just a dream. Whew!" Now imagine yourself waking up the next day, discovering you've paid twice as much as you should have for an item or wrote a check for an item that was in poor condition? Now that's a nightmare that will never go away!

Cards Versus Memorabilia: Which Is Better?

An inexperienced collector might not see any difference between collecting sports cards and collecting sports memorabilia. The differences are as vast as those between football and baseball. Yes, you are collecting an item related to a sport or team or athlete. Collectors come in all shapes, sizes, ages, and colors. That's one reason mastering the search function is a wonderful thing. The best thing to do is to collect what you like: You may be stuck with it forever! Far be it from me to advise you what to collect. That should come from your heart.

Both sports cards and sports autographs have professional grading standards. Companies charge a fee to authenticate the condition of sports collectibles. Some terminology surrounding cards and memorabilia sounds similar, but rest assured that differences exist. For example, if you buy a card in what is accepted as mint condition, that usually describes an item that is a 9 on a scale of 1 to 10, with 10 being best. That same mint description regarding other memorabilia can translate into something completely different: The item is in mint condition but the signature is not. Or perhaps the signature is in mint condition and the item is not.

Some card collectors value only rookie cards. Some value the football card market. Others choose baseball or hockey or basketball—simply ignore current offerings and concentrate on what is commonly referred to as vintage cards. Vintage cards were manufactured in the 1970s or earlier.

Other collectors may disdain cards altogether, instead searching out autographed items pertaining to one sport, or one team, or one athlete. Collectors come in all shapes, sizes, ages, and colors, and that is why the eBay Search is a wonderful thing to master. As advised previously, the best thing to do is to follow your heart and collect what you like—you may be stuck with it forever!

Other collectors search out autographed items pertaining to one sport, one team, or one athlete. Autograph and memorabilia collectors love to obtain the mint item, judged to be in perfect (or as perfect as possible) condition.

chapter 4

Authentication Is Sweeping the Nation

I will start by saying that whether you choose to authenticate or grade your sports collectible is strictly up to you. A lot of people think it's a bunch of hooey. "I've never, ever bought a graded card," they might say, "and I'm not about to start right now." That is fine, but the truth of the matter is that card grading and memorabilia authentication are no longer fads. They've evolved and become the rule, not the exception. Truth be told, with authentication sweeping the nation, selling non-graded cards will probably get tougher in the future. It's that popular these days.

Generally speaking, there are two distinct processes involved in this area:

1. **Authentication:** Determining whether an item is genuine, based on an independent authenticator's physical inspection.

2. **Grading:** Determining the physical condition of an item.

While authentication involves whether or not an item is even "real," grading is also a vital process. With collectibles, condition can be as important, or more so, than scarcity in many cases.

Several well-known companies exist solely to provide authentication and/or grading services for collectors. These services are provided to protect buyers, too. As with any industry or endeavor where huge sums of money are involved, the number of fakes and cheats seems to grow every day. If you want to spend a few hundred dollars on that last, expensive card to complete your set or collection, you don't want to find out years later that some unscrupulous person has trimmed the edges to improve its appearance—or worse yet, printed a bogus card and absconded with your money! This is another good reason to heed my "Do your homework" advice and to keep up on trends and news. Familiarize yourself with people and you learn who to trust and whom to stay away from.

Watch Out for That "Foul Ball"!

When an athlete makes headlines, you can bet some wise guy out there thinks he can illegally make a buck off of it—and get away with it. Probably the most forged sports autographs of recent times were those of Joe DiMaggio and Mickey Mantle. More recently, the home run-hitting exploits of San Francisco Giants' slugger Barry Bonds have spawned fake autographs on the collectibles market; see Figure 4.1. Only a few years before Bonds broke Mark McGwire's single-season home run record with 73 round-trippers in 2001, you could've had a Bonds signature on a baseball (and a real autograph, at that) for $30 or so. As Bonds continues closing in on Hank Aaron's all-time mark of 755 career homers, the retail value of an authentic Bonds autographed baseball has climbed to $500. (And Bonds has opted out of the Major League Players Association contract to market his signed collectibles on his own through www .BarryBonds.com.) A forger knows he can make more money by faking a Barry Bonds autograph than one of most other players, so my advice is for the buyer to beware: If the price seems too good to be true, it probably is!

The FBI's Approach

Even the Federal Bureau of Investigation got involved in sports memorabilia a few years ago. In the 1990s, the FBI's Chicago division began a sports memorabilia fraud investigation. That investigation targeted individuals who forged, fraudulently authenticated, and distributed Chicago athletes' autographed memorabilia (including, of course, Michael Jordan memorabilia). Operation Foul Ball led to details that helped suggest the fraud problem might be nationwide. Even some items that include a Certificate of Authenticity (basically, a piece of paper serving as a written guarantee that an item is real) aren't necessarily authentic, according to the investigation.

Figure 4.1

Can you spot which baseball pictured here has the real Barry Bonds autograph on it? The one on the left might look authentic, but the hologram attached to the ball on the right gives it away.

The FBI claims that while it's impossible to precisely estimate the percentage of forged memorabilia, possibly more than half of the autographed memorabilia is forged. In fact, some memorabilia experts claim that up to 90 percent of the market is forged. Industry experts estimate that the autographed memorabilia market in the United States is approximately $1 billion per year. Using these estimates, forged memorabilia comprises between $500,000,000 and $900,000,000 of the market.

The FBI's earlier findings led to another investigation in 1997 called Operation Bullpen. Using help from San Diego Padres star Tony Gwynn and St. Louis

Cardinals slugger Mark McGwire, the FBI's San Diego division built on information gathered from Operation Foul Ball and the Upper Deck Company to institute an undercover operation designed to infiltrate a nationwide memorabilia fraud network. Gwynn and McGwire helped the FBI by identifying forgeries of their autographs. To help increase public awareness of this memorabilia fraud problem, the FBI came up with these suggestions:

■ **If the price is too good to be true, it is probably a fake.** If a company offers an autographed item well below competitors' prices and market value, be wary. An example includes Michael Jordan basketballs, which some companies sell for as low as $150.00. Given Jordan's current exclusive contract with Upper Deck and difficulties associated with obtaining his autograph, the *Tuff Stuff Magazine* market value of an autographed Jordan Basketball is $500. Upper Deck Michael Jordan autographed basketballs retail for up to $1,500. (Caution: A high price does not by any means suggest authenticity, either.)

■ **Certificates of authenticity are not guarantees of authenticity.** Individuals and companies involved with selling forged memorabilia often include a Certificate of Authenticity, allegedly from a third-party expert. Often, the authenticator is either a knowing participant in the fraud or unknowing but incompetent. Carefully read the Certificate of Authenticity, looking for the authentication language, an address or telephone number, and name of the authenticators. Do not accept copies of Certificates of Authenticity.

■ **A photograph of an athlete or celebrity signing an autograph is not a guarantee of authenticity.** This investigation revealed that it is a common practice of forged memorabilia traffickers to include a photograph of the athlete/celebrity signing the item along with a Certificate of Authenticity. Traffickers also include photographs of themselves with the athlete/celebrity to lend credibility to their forged memorabilia.

■ **An individual or company having a paid signing session with an athlete or celebrity is no guarantee of authenticity.** Operation Bullpen has revealed that forged memorabilia traffickers mix forged memorabilia with items signed during an autograph session. For example, a company may pay to have an athlete sign 500 items. After the signing, the company mixes forgeries with the authentic autographs. The company also may continue selling forged items after the authentic items have been sold, claiming that they were from the autograph session. That is why most major sports memorabilia companies (Upper Deck Authenticated, TriStar Productions, Steiner Sports, Mounted Memories, etc.) began including their own tamper-proof foil holograms on items from their signings with many high-profile athletes. An item with no hologram, but with a Certificate of Authenticity, has become a rare thing these days.

■ **The memorabilia selling method should not affect skepticism about the item's authenticity.** The investigation revealed that traffickers sell their forgeries through a variety of methods that may lend credibility. One such sales method is through charity auctions in which the trafficker splits the profits with the charity. At charity auctions, buyers often overpay for items and do not question authenticity. Traffickers also sell forged items through trade publications, television shopping networks, trade shows, retail businesses, and the Internet.

■ **Before purchasing autographed memorabilia—especially "vintage" or deceased athlete/celebrity memorabilia—ask questions about the history and circumstances relating to the autograph.** Be wary of far-fetched or elaborate stories that are difficult, if not impossible, to verify. Common false stories suggest connections to an athlete, or "runners" employed to get autographs. Whenever possible, attempt to verify the history and circumstances of the autographed items before making the purchase.

■ **Send a request for an autograph directly to the athlete's team.** Include a self-addressed, stamped envelope or container and letter requesting that the enclosed item be autographed. Only send photographs, cards, or balls. Don't send large items such as bats and jerseys. In the letter requesting an autograph, request information relating to where you can purchase authentic autographed items if the athlete does not sign autographs through mailed requests. The athlete or team may direct you to a company that has an autograph contract with the athlete.

■ **Dealing directly with the athlete's company or an exclusive contract company greatly reduces the likelihood of purchasing forged memorabilia.** To counter the forged memorabilia problem, many athletes and celebrities are either creating their own autograph company or signing exclusive contracts with specific sports memorabilia companies. Just like Upper Deck or Steiner, many of the bigger-name athletes of today's generation (such as Bonds and Jerry Rice) and some of those from the past (such as Willie Mays and Joe Montana) have developed patented foil holograms that are tamper-proof. An unscrupulous buyer or seller who tries to remove these holograms will discover that these authentication devices are designed to "flake" into several worthless pieces of tin foil. Not a good idea.

eBay's Approach

A list of some better-known culprits is available on the eBay site as a result of the FBI investigations. As a result of that case, eBay doesn't permit any Certificates of Authenticity on its site issued by these companies:

- All-Sports Cards & Memorabilia
- Classic Memorabilia
- Dave Niedema (a.k.a. Dave Madiema)
- Donald Frangipani
- Forensic Document Services-Robert Prouty
- Hollywood Dreams
- J. Dimaggio Co.
- Legends Sports Memorabilia
- North Shore Sports
- Pro Sports
- Pro Sports Memorabilia
- R.R.'s Sports Cards & Collectibles
- SCCA/Front Page Art Angela-John Marino
- Slamdunk Sportscards Memoribilia (note the company name's misspelling of "Memorabilia")
- Sport Card Kid Hunting Beachor
- Sports Management Group
- Sports Alley Memorabilia

- Sports Management Group

- Stan's Sports

- Stans Sports Memorabilia

- Steve Ryan

- Universal

- Universal Inc.

- Universal Memorabilia

- W.W. Sportscards & Collectibles

In an unrelated matter, eBay publicizes the fact it has learned that hundreds of Certificates of Authenticity originally issued by autograph authenticator Donald Frangipani had been fraudulently copied or altered. eBay also banned items bearing Certificates of Authenticity from forensic examiner Robert Prouty and a company known as Forensic Document Services, based on information from the New York Department of Consumer Affairs and federal law enforcement, due to "limited reviews . . . not sufficient to provide meaningful assurances about the authenticity of the autograph. As a number of items issued with such certificates may be forgeries . . . ."

Best advice to cull from all of this is to know your seller. Consider these questions:

- Can he tell you from where the item came?

- Can he produce a valid Certificate of Authenticity that comes with a money-back guarantee?

- Has he sold to others on eBay without any issues of authenticity clouding his feedback rating?

Red flags should go up anytime you're thinking about making a purchase if:

- A seller has little or no feedback.

- He offers a bargain deal on something valuable.

- He cannot provide provenance or photos of the item for sale.

Players' Approaches

Several athletes, Bonds included, have developed personal holograms to put on autographed items. With the latest innovations, most of these holograms are made of a special foil-like product that can only be applied to an item once. Should someone try to remove the hologram, they usually flake into small pieces that prevents them from being reused. Jerry Rice, Joe Montana, Willie Mays, Sammy Sosa, and several other big-name athletes also have begun putting their trademark holograms on signed products to help collectors know if the item they are purchasing is real. Most of the larger memorabilia companies—Upper Deck Authenticated, Steiner Sports, TriStar Productions, and Mounted Memories—have developed hologram systems. The systems have become popular with collectors who have grown weary of hearing about the fakes and cheats who have ripped off some buyers. You often pay a bit more for a product that includes this hologram authentication process, but that's the cost of peace of mind.

How Do I Know if My Item Makes the Grade?

When it comes to collecting sports cards, the two biggest accepted grading companies are Beckett and Professional Sports Authenticator (PSA, a division of Collectors Universe, one of the leading names in collectibles authentication). Which one is best? As they say, beauty is in the eye of the beholder. Each has its followers, each has its detractors, and each has its own grading standards and pricing structures. If you pick up the latest issue of *Beckett Baseball* magazine, for example, market prices vary between the two grading systems. A mint rookie card for Ken Griffey, Jr. theoretically might be worth $100 today if Beckett (BGS) graded it Gem Mint; however, it might be worth a few dollars more or less if PSA graded and encapsulated it. Publications such as *Beckett Baseball* and *Sports Collectors Digest* offer pricing guides that can help collectors know the "high" and the "low" market values of cards, as well as the going rate for memorabilia (photos, balls, jerseys, etc.) autographed by their favorite athletes (see Figure 4.2). Usually, it depends on a collector's own preference. Some like PSA better than BGS, while others are exactly the opposite. And if you started a collection of PSA-graded cards years ago, you might want to maintain the PSA link. Beauty is in the eye of the beholder.

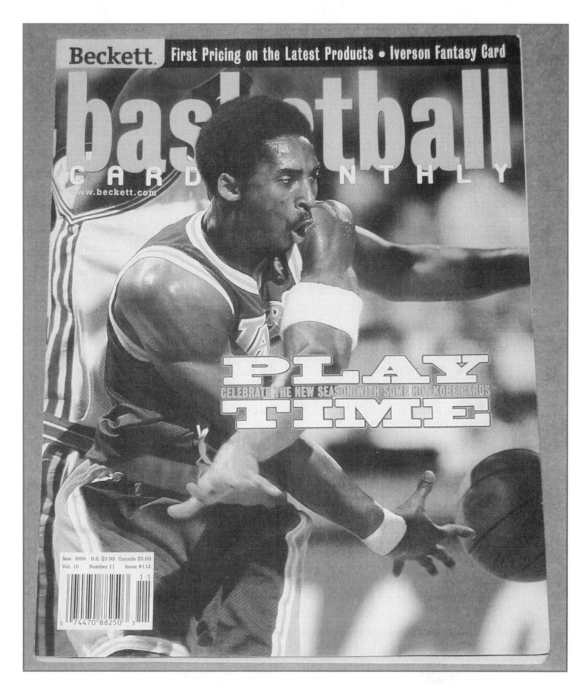

Figure 4.2

Price guides such as *Beckett* magazine provide buyers with a basis for price and value comparison.

Grading is a way of determining the physical condition of an item, such as "poor quality" or "mint condition." The actual grading system depends on the type of item being graded. Trading cards that have been professionally graded are encapsulated in a plastic or acrylic holder and labeled with the card set identification and grade before being returned to the owner. A typical graded trading card would include a sticker that reveals the grade (e.g., PSA 9 Mint), along with the year, company, and card number (e.g., 1975 Topps #1).

Authentication is a way of determining whether an item is genuine and described appropriately. Because of their training and experience, experts can often detect counterfeits from subtle details. However, you should know that two expert authenticators may differ on the authenticity of the same item.

Authentication and grading services can help a potential buyer evaluate an item before bidding on it. For a small fee, an independent, experienced evaluator can help examine a listing on eBay and point out potential problems with an autograph. Buyers can also use these authentication and grading services to get a thorough evaluation of a recently purchased item or one they had autographed in person at a card show or at the ballpark.

PSA offers a QuickOpinion™ service through eBay for $7.49. You can reach the web site at http://www.psadna.com/quickopinion. This service enables you to get an opinion from one of the autograph industry's leading authenticators as to the genuineness of an item being offered for sale on eBay, providing you with valuable knowledge and helping you make informed buying decisions. The PSA/DNA link will take you through the process of entering the eBay item number for the autographed item you might bid on and providing a credit card number for the $7.49 payment. Then, the item listing page will be forwarded via email to one of PSA/DNA's qualified experts for an online examination. A determination is promised within 36 hours, but usually the response is received sooner than that. The customer receives an email from PSA/DNA regarding whether the online authenticator believes the item is "likely genuine" or "likely not genuine."

■ **Likely genuine:** The expert believes that the item, if physically submitted to Collectors Universe's PSA/DNA division for examination, would likely receive a PSA/DNA Certificate of Authenticity.

- **Likely not genuine:** The expert believes that the item, if physically submitted to PSA/DNA for examination, would likely not receive a PSA/DNA Certificate of Authenticity.

Should you decide to use this service, don't wait until the last day of the auction. By then, it's too late.

If QuickOpinion is unable to render an opinion, your payment will be refunded. There are several reasons an opinion might not be possible:

1. **Bad photos:** The scanned images of the item are inadequate (e.g., image too small, poor focus, bad lighting).

2. **Lack of expertise:** While PSA/DNA experts are some of the best in their field, they cannot authenticate the signature of every personality, in *every* field/sport, throughout all of history. If the item bears the signature of an extremely obscure sports figure, PSA/DNA acknowledges it may not be possible to authenticate the autograph.

If you are the successful bidder and ultimately purchase the item, you have the option to physically send it to PSA/DNA for a formal and complete examination. If you do that within 90 days of the close of the auction, you will be entitled to a credit of $7.49 off the regular authentication price. After the in-person examination, you would receive a formal Letter of Authenticity from PSA/DNA should the item pass inspection.

If you need a professional opinion on your item's authenticity or condition, eBay has links to companies that provide this specialized service (see Figure 4.3). These links are available at http://pages.ebay.com/help/community/auth-overview.html. The companies found here are associated with eBay in that they provide a valuable service to buyers and sellers. However, each company also is a strong entity unto itself, and does a lot of business in the buying/selling community away from eBay, too. Their links to eBay should tell you they are companies eBay has found trustworthy and worthy of being associated with eBay in the first place. The services they provide—professional authentication and positive condition evaluation—can substantially increase your collectible's value. Of course, these services cost a fee, which can range from less than $10 (having a card graded, for instance) to more than $100 (to have an autograph or a piece of game-used equipment authenticated, for example).

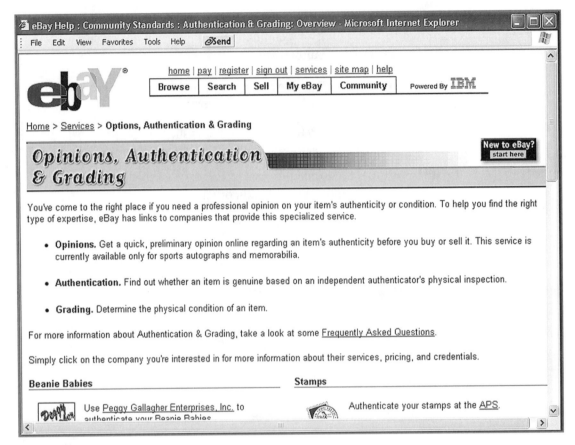

Figure 4.3

eBay can link you with professional services to grade or authenticate your collectible.

Trading Cards

So, where do you turn if you want to find out if your trading cards make the grade? There are several options available, but some of the best include Professional Sports Authenticator (PSA), Sportscard Guaranty (SCG), and Global Authentication, Inc. (GAI).

PSA

PSA is widely regarded as a pioneer in the field of trading card grading, and is held in high esteem by buyers and sellers alike. This is the place that can verify the authenticity and quality of the trading cards you buy and sell online. With this site (www.psacard.com), you have direct access to PSA's expert grading and authentication services. When you submit your cards to PSA, some of the top trading card grading experts in the world see your cards. Each card is examined by a minimum of three independent experts for grade and authenticity. PSA experts evaluate a card's physical condition based on the 10-point PSA grading scale (10 being best or Gem Mint). Cards graded by PSA are encapsulated in a sonically sealed, tamper-evident holder with a certification tag describing the card and the physical condition (the grade).

PSA experts also examine trading cards for authenticity. PSA will not encapsulate cards that bear evidence of trimming, recoloring, restoration, or any other forms of tampering. When you own a card in a PSA holder, you know that experts have verified that it is genuine. The PSA grading system is widely respected and has been supported by professional dealers, collectors, and leading auction firms since 1991.

SGC

SGC is similar to PSA, but offers grading on a scale of 1 to 100. For collectors who desire a more specific grading scale, SGC (www.sgccard.com) employs one designed to eliminate the tweeners (not quite a Mint 9 yet a bit better than an 8.5 grade). SGC employs this method because it believes it's a more accurate and consistent grading scale, which can mean more accurate prices for your sports cards. The following are example grades from their scale:

100 PRISTINE: A virtually flawless card. 50/50 centering, crisp focus, four sharp corners, free of stains, no breaks in surface gloss, no print or refractor lines, and no visible wear under magnification.

98 GEM 10: 55/45 or better centering, sharp focus, four sharp corners, free of stains, no breaks in surface gloss, no print or refractor lines, and no visible wear. A slight print spot visible under close scrutiny is allowable if it does not detract from the aesthetics of the card.

96 MINT 9: 60/40 or betting centering, sharp focus, and four sharp corners. A minor flaw may exist upon close examination. A minor flaw may be but is not limited to: a slight nick to one corner, a small gloss break or surface scratch, a minor print line or minor refractor line, a minor focus or color imperfection, or a small print spot.

92 NM/MT+ 8.5: 65/35 or better centering, four sharp corners. A few minor flaws may exist upon close examination. A minor flaw may be but is not limited to: a slight nick to one corner, a small gloss break or surface scratch, a minor print line or minor refractor line, a minor focus or color imperfection, or a small print spot.

88 NM/MT 8: 65/35 or better centering, corners sharp to the naked eye but may exhibit slight wear under closer examination. A few small flaws may exist upon close examination. A small flaw may be but is not limited to: very minor wear on one corner, a gloss break or surface scratch, a print line or refractor line, a focus or color imperfection, or a print spot.

86 NM+ 7.5: 70/30 or better centering, a few small flaws may exist upon close examination. A small flaw may be but is not limited to: very minor wear on one corner, a gloss break or surface scratch, a print line or refractor line, a focus or color imperfection, or a print spot.

84 NRMT 7: 70/30 or better centering, slight wear on some corners, minor scratching, some print spots or speckling, and print lines or refractor lines are acceptable. Card may exhibit a slightly skewed (diamond) cut.

80 EX/NM 6: 75/25 or better centering, slight fuzzing of corners may be evident, skewed cut may be more evident, focus or register may be off, and slight notching of edges may exist.

70 EX+ 5.5: A 60 EX 5 card with higher-grade centering or corners.

60 EX 5: 80/20 or better centering, minor rounding or fuzzing of corners, roughness or chipping along edge (no layering), one very slight surface (spider) crease may exist on one side of the card, gloss may be lost from surface with some scratching that does not detract from the aesthetics of the card.

50 VG/EX 4: 85/15 or better centering, corners are slightly rounded with modest surface wear. Light hairline crease may show on one or both sides. A light tear or surface break may exist.

40 VG 3: 90/10 or better centering, corners more rounded but not excessive, stronger creasing may exist. Poorer focus, registration, and discoloration, and staining are more noticeable.

30 GOOD 2: Centered 90/10 or better. This card usually exhibits one or more of these characteristics: heavy print spots, heavy crease(s), pinhole(s), color or focus imperfections or discoloration, surface scuffing or tear, rounded and/or fraying corners, ink or pencil marking(s), and lack of all or some original gloss.

20 FAIR 1.5: Centered 90/10 or better. This card usually exhibits several of these characteristics: heavy print spots, heavy crease(s), pinhole(s), color or focus imperfections or discoloration, surface scuffing or tears, rounded and/or fraying corners, ink or pencil marking(s), and lack of all or some original gloss, a small portion of the card may be missing.

10 POOR 1: This card usually exhibits many of these characteristics: heavy print spots, heavy crease(s), pinhole(s), color or focus imperfections or discoloration, surface scuffing or tears, rounded and/or fraying corners, ink or pencil marking(s), and lack of all or some original gloss, small portions of the card may be missing.

GAI

GAI is one of the newer card grading companies (www.gacard.net). Similar to PSA, GAI utilizes a grading scale of 1 to 10, with 10 being best, and includes half-point increments to help designate tweeners. Global not only grades trading cards, but also began the art of grading unopened material such as wax packs or boxes of cards. Interestingly enough, an unopened pack of 1954 Topps hockey cards sold for a reported $6,500 after grading out at GAI 7.

Sports Autographs and Memorabilia

PSA/DNA is affiliated with the same PSA card grading service that's linked to the eBay site. PSA/DNA is perhaps the most well-known and well-regarded autograph authentication service in the world. This is where you can have your valuable vintage autographs certified by the world's leading experts. With this site (www.psadna.com) you have direct access to PSA/DNA's expert third-party autograph certification service. When your autographed items are submitted to PSA/DNA, they are examined by the world's leading autograph experts. After they have been certified by PSA/DNA, collectors know that the industry's top experts are convinced your autograph is authentic. Each autograph is examined by at least three of PSA/DNA's autograph experts. After each autograph has been certified, it is DNA tagged with a synthetic, invisible trace liquid. A tamper-evident label displaying a serialized certification number is applied and a Certificate of Authenticity is issued.

Once applied, the authenticating mark is permanent, nondamaging, nontransferable, and nearly impossible to replicate. The chances are 1 in 33 trillion that someone would be able to randomly re-create the exact sequence of the DNA strand that is used for the PSA/DNA tag. The clear liquid that contains the DNA tag applied to your autographed item is invisible and nondamaging and the unique certification number can verify the history of any PSA/DNA-certified item simply by calling PSA/DNA customer service or via the company's web site.

PSA/DNA has been used exclusively to help authenticate memorabilia connected to many historical events and achievements:

- **Mark McGwire 70th home run ball:** On October 7, 1998, at the St. Louis Cardinals Hall of Fame, PSA/DNA was entrusted with the authentication of the most significant sports item of the decade: the Mark McGwire 70th home run ball, which sold at auction in 1999 for $3.005 million.

- **Hank Aaron's record-breaking 715th home run baseball and bat:** On April 2, 1999, at the Atlanta Braves Hall of Fame Museum, PSA/DNA tagged Hall of Famer Hank Aaron's record-breaking 715th home run baseball and the bat he used to hit it.

- **McFarlane Collection:** On June 3, 1999, at Dodger Stadium, PSA/DNA authenticated the McFarlane Collection, which consists of some of Mark McGwire's home run balls (1, 63, 64, 67, 68, 69, and 70 [which was reauthenticated]) and an assortment of Sammy Sosa's home run balls (33, 61, and 66).

OnlineAuthentics.com provides an online registry database that enables manufacturers of autographed sports memorabilia to register items that they produce. All registered items are assigned a unique ID number, which allows item verification via the Internet. The database also includes a text description of the item (what type, when it was signed, company of origin) and an image of that exact signed item. OnlineAuthentics.com also allows eBay users to submit listings of celebrity signed collectibles to their team of industry leaders and receive confidential opinions via email within 36 hours. Like PSA and GAI, Online-Authentics.com offers an online database through which a Certificate of Authenticity and the matching registration number can be authenticated right on your computer.

Who Do You Trust?

One of the best pieces of advice you'll find in this book is this: Check out the seller's or buyer's record of eBay feedback. If you were going to buy a new suit for a wedding, you probably would search for not only the suit you were looking for at the best price, but for a suit broker you could trust. It's extremely unlikely you would look for that suit at the local swap meet (unless looking good was unimportant to you!); so why would you trust buying something on eBay if you didn't know something about the seller you are dealing with, too?

There's a reason every eBay user has a number inside parentheses after his name. That's his eBay feedback rating. Get to know it well, since this is how eBay polices itself. A low score means the user is fairly new to eBay; a high feedback score means the opposite. He's been around a while and has done dozens (or hundred, or thousands) of transactions over the months and years. By clicking a user's feedback rating, you can see how many positive or negative feedbacks he has received over the past month, the past 6 months, or the past 12 months. The feedback record is color coordinated: green is good, red is bad. You find an overall feedback percentage (for example, 99.8 percent positive feedback) and how many different members left feedback overall for this user. If 3,000 different users have left 5,000 positive feedbacks for a seller, simple math shows you that 2,000 different users have made multiple purchases from this seller. That is usually a good sign!

Clicking the Feedback Forum tab lets you know this is the place to learn about your trading partners. View their reputations and express your opinions by leaving feedback on your transactions. According to eBay itself, "such member-to-member comments help the millions of buyers and sellers in the community build trust and share their trading experiences with others."

When eBay was just six months old, the community had already grown to several hundred members. Realizing the importance of having a simple and powerful way for members to exchange experiences, eBay's founder launched the Feedback Forum.

Every eBay member has a profile in the Feedback Forum. A profile has basic information about the member and a list of feedback left by their trading partners from previous transactions. Learning to trust a community member has a lot to do with what their past customers or sellers have to say.

For each transaction, only the buyer and seller can rate each other by leaving feedback (see Figure 4.4). Each feedback consists of a positive, negative, or neutral rating and a short comment. Leaving honest comments about a particular eBay member gives other community members a good idea what to expect when dealing with that member. Once it is left, the feedback becomes a permanent part of the member's profile.

Feedback ratings determine each member's feedback score. A positive rating adds 1 to the score, a negative rating decreases it by 1, and a neutral rating has no impact. The higher the feedback score, the more positive ratings they've received. However, a member can increase or decrease another member's score by only 1 no matter how many transactions they share.

Any seller worth dealing with, and spending your hard-earned cash with, will guarantee the authenticity of her item. That includes getting your money back should a subsequent authentication attempt to prove that the item she sold you is damaged or not real. That is why incorporating the feedback system is important if you want to buy or sell on eBay.

If you're running into a bit of trouble with a buyer or seller, don't be too hasty to leave negative feedback. Try to do everything you can to contact the person. You never know if someone has gone away a few days on vacation or for business, or if their email provider has gone on the fritz. Better to give someone the benefit of the doubt (unless a poor track record reveals serious prior problems) than to regret it later on.

Similarly, most eBay users don't mind it if you email them with questions about their experiences with past buyers or sellers. You can email them for details about a previous transaction with a user you might be thinking of doing business with; the worst they can do is say no to your request.

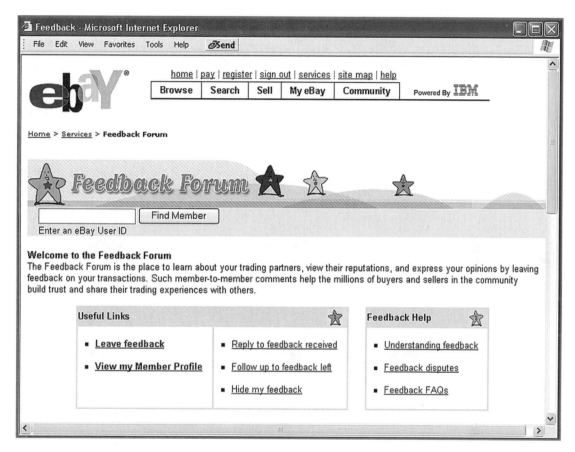

Figure 4.4

The eBay feedback system gives buyers and sellers a way to rate transactions. It's a good way to see if you can trust a fellow auction trader.

What exactly are your options, should you run into someone disreputable? One of eBay's foremost stated goals is to work closely with members of its community to ensure a safe trading environment. Don't get the wrong idea: Most eBay sellers are dependable, friendly people who want to earn your repeat business. Just like the rest of the world, however, there are bound to be a few rotten apples in the barrel.

If you detect suspicious activity by an unscrupulous seller, he may be guilty of violating the eBay user agreement under the seller non-performance policy. If a seller does not deliver an item for which payment was accepted, or has significantly misrepresented an item in an auction, then it could be time to contact eBay or take additional steps. If you're unsuccessful at reaching your seller by email or by telephone, or you've reported your problem to eBay and still have no resolution, you have a couple more alternatives. Try dispute resolution through a third party. Many buyers or sellers who have a problem they can't solve themselves often employ SquareTrade (see Figure 4.5), but this must be done within the first 30 days after an auction is completed.

Figure 4.5

SquareTrade can serve as an independent third party to help resolve disputes between buyers and sellers.

Here's how to use SquareTrade to resolve a dispute.

1. *File a case.*

   On the SquareTrade web site (www.squaretrade.com), a buyer or seller clicks File a Case and fills out a short online form designed to identify the problem and its possible resolutions.

2. *SquareTrade notifies the other party.*

   SquareTrade contacts the other party via an automatically generated email and provides instruction on responding to the case. The case and all related responses appear on a password-protected case page on the SquareTrade web site.

3. *The parties discuss their issues directly in direct negotiation.*

   Once each party is aware of the issues, they first try to reach an agreement using SquareTrade's direct negotiation tool. This initial phase of the service is a completely automated, web-based communications tool and is currently free of charge to all users. Using SquareTrade's secure case page, the parties try to reach an agreement by communicating directly with each other.

   The other option is to have a SquareTrade mediator guide the process. If the parties cannot resolve the case through direct negotiation, they can request the assistance of a SquareTrade mediator. The mediator's role is to facilitate positive, solution-oriented discussion between the parties. He or she does not act as a judge or arbitrator. The mediator only recommends a resolution if the parties request it.

4. *The case is resolved.*

   The parties may reach a settlement agreement either independently during direct negotiation or with the assistance of a SquareTrade mediator.

SquareTrade can't force a party to participate. However, if you ever find yourself contacted by SquareTrade in regards to a dispute, it is probably in your best interests to respond. If you do not, the other party may pursue a few options. For example, if the other party requested feedback removal or withdrawal as part of the case, and you do not respond, then the feedback might be removed or withdrawn anyway in accordance with eBay's Feedback Removal or Withdrawal Policy. The other party may also pursue claims through insurance, credit card charge backs, or legal processes that may cost you more time and money. In the end, if you do not respond, it can affect your reputation in the marketplace.

Most purchases on eBay are protected by a program that depends on how you paid (or were paid) for your item.

- If you paid via PayPal, your item may have enhanced protection through PayPal buyer protection. When you pay for a qualified listing with PayPal, this program provides coverage up to $500 at no additional cost. To see if an item is covered, look for the Seller Information section on the listing and confirm the item's eligibility. Most other items are covered up to $200 (minus a $25 processing fee) under eBay's buyer protection program

- If you paid via credit card, contact your credit card company. Most issuers provide 100 percent online protection.

Even if you paid by check or money order, you still have options. You can file a fraud alert with eBay. For most items, the eBay standard purchase protection program provides partial reimbursement for losses resulting from non-delivery or misrepresentation up to $200 (minus $25 processing cost).

If you sent payment and did not receive your item or you received an item that the seller significantly misrepresented, eBay encourages you to file a Fraud Alert. Buyers can file a Fraud Alert at least 30 days but not more than 60 days after a listing's end date. Please keep in mind that in addition to filing a Fraud Alert, you can contact eBay to report fraud at any time by following the steps on the Buyer Protection Program page (http://pages.ebay.com/help/confidence/isgw-fraud-protection.html). The Fraud Alert acts as:

1. An online forum for buyers and sellers to resolve transaction disputes.

2. A formal complaint filed with eBay regarding a seller's activities.

3. The initial step to file for reimbursement through eBay's Buyer Protection Program.

In some situations, when you can't contact the other party or the other party refuses to deal with you, you may want to contact law enforcement to report suspicious activity. To do so, you can file a complaint with the Internet Fraud Complaint Center at www.ifccfbi.gov/index.asp or visit the Federal Trade Commission's web site at www.consumer.gov/idtheft/. You may also want to contact a law enforcement agency in your location or the seller's or buyer's location.

chapter 5

Getting Ready to Bid

When you feel an urge to start bidding, it's a good idea to figure out how serious you are about an item. Do you want to buy the item, no matter the price? Are you just looking to buy something for less than the most recent eBay sales price on record? Or are you just looking for a really good deal, a bargain that you can't pass up?

How quickly do you need the item? Do you need it right away as a gift for a friend or family member or are you willing to wait a few days—or a few weeks or months, for that matter? Does the seller's feedback matter or are you willing to take a chance on an eBay newbie who has no track record? If a seller has a recent negative feedback, will that be enough to preclude you from doing business with him?

Are there similar auctions (or those with exactly the same item?) that close within the same 24 hours or week? Do shipping costs and shipping methods matter to you? What about how far the item must travel before it gets to you?

Ask yourself all these questions and answer (it is advisable not to do this aloud, lest someone think you have gone eBay-crazy) to develop some sort of basic bidding strategy before setting out on the long, winding, high-speed eBay highway. Otherwise, you very well could find yourself stuck in traffic, lost on a deserted road, sputtering along with no gas stations anywhere in sight to ask for directions.

If you collect sports memorabilia, undoubtedly you know all about the extensive planning that a professional franchise or college sports team goes through to map out a start-finish route to a season that hopefully ends with the satisfaction of winning a championship. Your favorite team sets its goals before training camp even gets started, then practices and prepares long and hard before finally putting its game plan into place. At that point, the team must follow that game plan to a T and with a single purpose in mind. Consider this: How did Red Auerbach, Bill Russell, and the rest of the Boston Celtics win all those NBA championships in the 1950s and '60s? They had a game plan, they followed it, and it worked.

You can consider this book your own personal eBay coach. It will help you establish a game plan with the eventual goal of becoming a champion of eBay. You're going to get in tip-top bidding shape, get those hand-eye coordination muscles limbered up adequately for the ultimate mouse-clicking performance, and fine-tune your mindset for spotting a bargain—or help you weed out an overpriced offering that is best left for some other unsuspecting soul.

In more serious terms, it's time to get you personally acquainted with how eBay works, outline some bidding strategies, reveal choices (and red flags) when you get outbid, and suggest some tips to keep your emotions from getting in the way of your ultimate goal.

Take It Out for a Spin!

So you've dotted all the i's and crossed all the t's. You're all signed up for eBay and PayPal (see Chapter 2, "Pledge Allegiance to eBay"). Insert the key, rev up the engine, and take a spin out of the eBay showroom, shall we? Buckle up!

As an example, pretend you are looking to buy a Magic Johnson autographed photo. Go to the eBay search page, type in Magic Johnson (see Figure 5.1), and click the Search button.

Now, you might come up with hundreds of items that match your search criteria. That wouldn't be unusual; Magic Johnson is an extremely popular athlete among fans and collectors alike, and his likeable personality and infectious smile have only increased his popularity since his retirement from basketball.

Mosey on over to the Matching Categories filter on the left side of the page. From there, click the Memorabilia link (under Sports Mem, Cards & Fan Shop) (see Figure 5.2).

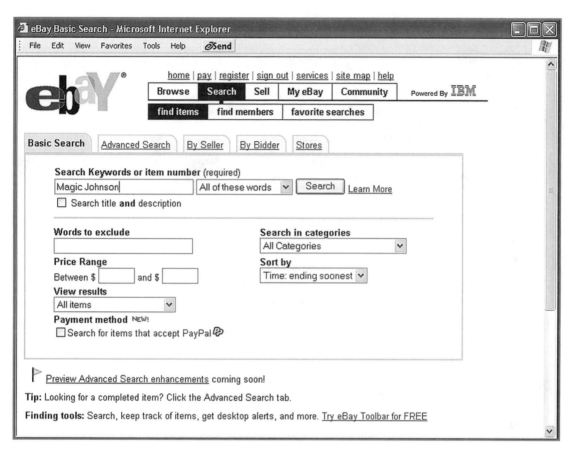

Figure 5.1

Go to the eBay search page and type in Magic Johnson.

By clicking on "Memorabilia," you have weeded out everything that matches Magic Johnson but is not listed under Memorabilia, which is the most likely category for a signed photograph. This is not to say that some sellers might mistakenly list their Magic Johnson autographed 8×10 photos under Cards or another category, but most seasoned sellers who know what they are doing and want to reach the largest customer base are usually certain to locate the correct spot in which to sell their wares.

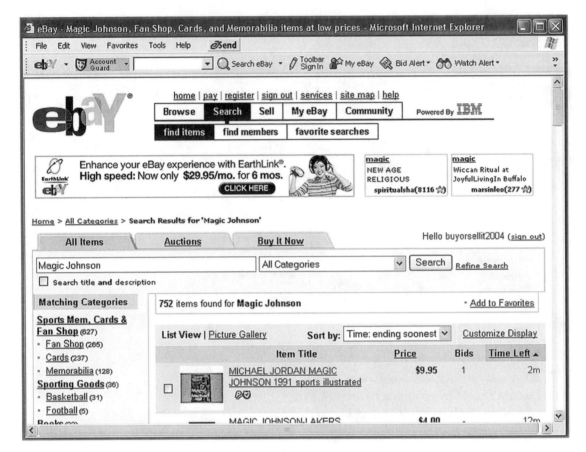

Figure 5.2

Click Memorabilia under Sports Mem, Cards & Fan Shop.

Your search now should be narrowed down from several hundred items to one hundred or so items (see Figure 5.3), depending on any particular day on eBay.

At this point you still have a few more options. You can opt to browse through the sale items just by scrolling up and down the eBay page on your screen or you can do a bit more sorting. What you decide to do depends on how familiar you are with and comfortable you feel using eBay. Now you've carefully maneuvered out of the showroom, and even though your salesman is still right

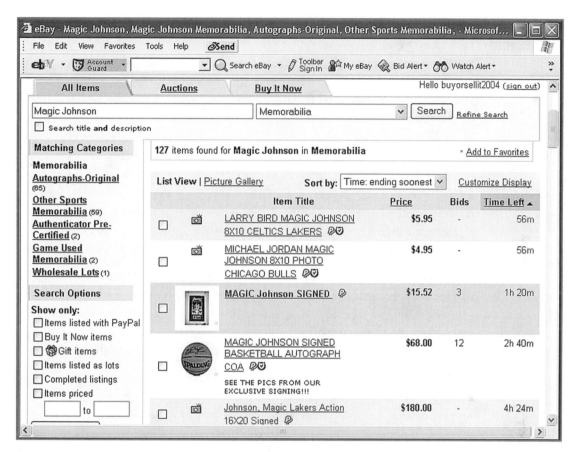

Figure 5.3

By narrowing your search, finding the item you want to buy is that much easier.

at your side, riding along in the back seat, you have the freedom to choose which way to go—turn left, turn right, go straight, whatever. You still have to watch out for the speeding cars (other bidders) all around you on the Information Superhighway, and you need to cautiously watch for red lights that might tell you to stop what you are doing—but indeed, you are at the controls now.

Ready to do some serious driving?

Picking the Right Road

Back to your search. You have a screen full of items that include Magic Johnson in the title description. What you are looking at is eBay's List view and its automatic default sort is set at Time: ending soonest. You are seeing items listed in the Memorabilia category that include Magic Johnson in the title, listed according to the auctions' end times. The auctions that will be completed soonest are at the top of your screen, and they might have only a few minutes to go before they end. Further down the screen, the end times increase in range from a few hours to a few days from now. This is usually the way beginners learn to move around eBay when they are searching for an item to purchase. If you want to just get bidding and see how well you can do against other users, this is the most simple approach.

However, say you are looking for a bargain, as most people are wont to do. It doesn't matter about the details; you just want to buy a Magic Johnson autographed item and you want to spend as little money as possible. The next step would be to click the arrow in the sort area and change the sort definition from Time: ending soonest to Price: lowest first. That will change the display on your screen, as you can see in Figure 5.4.

Now, let's say you want to actually see photos of the items you can bid on. This is particularly helpful when you are looking for something specific (for instance, a signed 8 x 10 photo) and you don't want to read hundreds and hundreds of lines of print on the computer screen to weed out everything else. They say a picture is worth a thousand words, and in this case, a picture can save you a thousand seconds of search time in some cases. To switch over to the Photo view from the List view, you need to click on the Picture Gallery tab that is found just to the left of the sort drop-down display that we just experimented with (see Figure 5.5). Now, you can see the thumbnail photos of the auctions that are included in the Picture Gallery. Scroll up and down the page to see the various offerings.

If you don't find anything to your liking on the first page, by the time you scroll down to the bottom of the screen, you'll find you can click the page display to move on to the next page of offerings; see Figure 5.6. The Page tab lets you skip to the next page of listings in the Picture Gallery (or to page 3, 4, 5, and so on).You can also add another word (for instance, "Lakers") into your Search

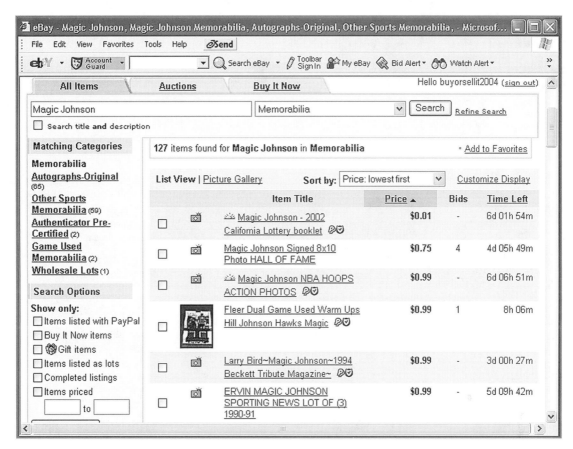

Figure 5.4

This sort will help you find the lowest prices on the items you are looking for.

requirements to help narrow down the field a bit. Remember: It's all up to you now, since you're doing the driving!

Assume you have been driving around a while, looking for a nice Magic Johnson item to bid on. You've come across a thumbnail photo that piques your interest and decide to click that listing for a closer look. Your pulse begins to quicken, your palms get moist, and you sit up a little taller in your chair—and up onto your computer screen comes a giant new display that puts you in a

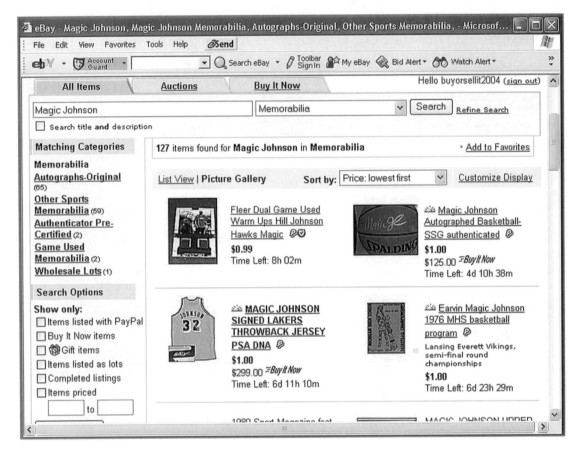

Figure 5.5

The Picture Gallery helps you see images of items up for sale.

neighborhood you've never driven through before. This just might be what you are looking for! See Figure 5.7 for your potentially fabulous find.

What you've found here might be an 8×10 photograph signed not only by Magic Johnson, but by Larry Bird, too! A very nice find, since it includes autographs from not only two Hall of Fame basketball players, but also two long-time friends and rivals—rivals who electrified fans when they played against each other in college (Magic at Michigan State, Bird at Indiana State) for the NCAA Championship and in the professional ranks of the National Basketball Association (Magic with the Los Angeles Lakers, Bird with the Boston Celtics).

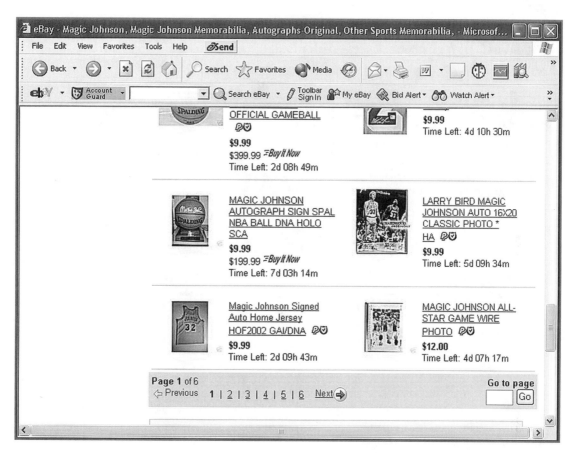

Figure 5.6

Use the Page tab to go on to page 2 and other pages that match what you are looking to bid on.

Even though you originally might have wanted to find a photo signed only by Magic, you have discovered a somewhat nicer item, and gee, isn't this one neat? That is the beauty, the magic, of eBay. Sometimes, just when you think you know exactly what you are looking for, you discover a whole new world out there. You find a new bend in the road—an item that is yours for the taking. At least it will be yours if the bid is right!

For this example, at least, assume you want to go ahead and bid on this item. First check the auction out a bit closer. Remember, you have to your homework!

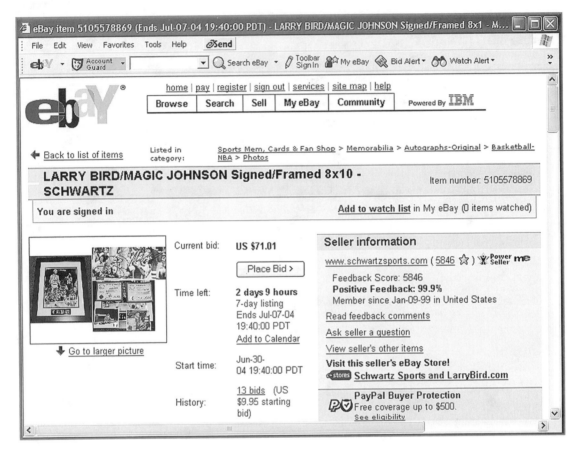

Figure 5.7

Our Search has resulted in finding this photo signed by both Magic Johnson and Larry Bird!

Read the Feedback

One of the first things to do is to check out the seller's reputation. In this example, the seller is Schwartz Sports Inc. with an eBay seller's feedback rating of 5846, which is a terrific testament to their base of satisfied customers. Still, if you haven't purchased an item from this seller before, it is a good idea to look a bit further into their feedback rating. Click the feedback rating in parentheses next to the seller's name. You can see such a rating in Figure 5.8.

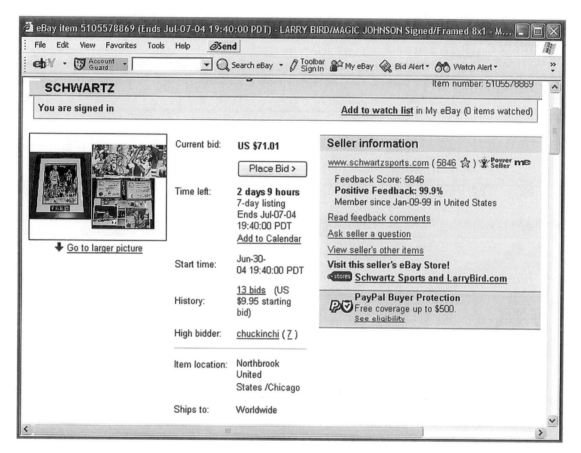

Figure 5.8

The feedback rating for a seller is located in the parentheses next to the seller's name.

The next screen that comes up gives you a closer look at Schwartz Sports Inc.'s track record with other buyers; see Figure 5.9. In this particular case, the screen shows that the seller has a 99.9 percent positive feedback rating, which is an extremely good sign and should give you reason to be at ease with this member of the eBay community. By scrolling down a bit further, you can see the positive (or negative) comments left by other buyers for this particular seller. The feedback remarks show the buyer's name and feedback rating, plus the date and item number of the transaction associated with that feedback rating.

Note

There is no set percentage of positive feedback to go by when making your decision. However, with the large quantity of offerings on eBay, a few simple clicks will help you compare one seller's track record with that of another. And oftentimes, that is enough for a buyer to pick one seller over another.

Keep in mind that the eBay feedback system is in no way perfect, but is the only system available to see how a seller has interacted with past buyers. If a seller has a rotten feedback record with negative comments from buyers who

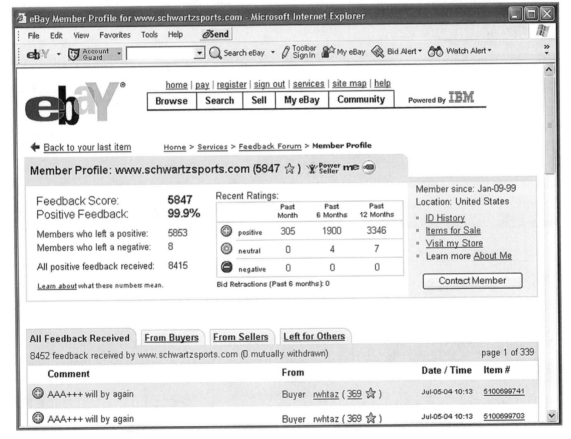

Figure 5.9

The feedback rating is a plus-minus system for which an eBay user gets a plus for every positive feedback and a minus for every negative feedback. There also are neutral comments that don't affect the feedback rating at all. This is a good place to choose whether to bid on a seller's items.

either received damaged goods or experienced slow shipping—or sometimes, received nothing at all for their money—that obviously is a good reason to avoid that particular seller. In this instance, however, Schwartz Sports' feedback (as of this transaction) was nearly as perfect as could be expected—keeping a 100 percent feedback rating on eBay is virtually impossible. There always will be a few buyers who never will be satisfied, no matter what a seller might do to appease a customer, but that is the nature of doing business. You can't please all the people all the time. But if you can please 99 percent of them on a regular basis, then you're doing a pretty darn good job!

Check Out the "Me" Page

Click the Back button at the top of your screen to return to the original item listing. Just to the right of the feedback number in parentheses, you find the Me icon for this seller. If you click that link, it takes you to a separate page where this eBay seller has provided information about himself or his company. In this case, you find more information about Schwartz Sports and its company background, along with some associated Internet links, a list of items they have up for sale, and possibly some recent feedback comments, too. See Figure 5.10.

After getting better acquainted with this fellow eBay user, click the Back button at the top of your screen one more time to return to the original item listing. At this point, you should read over the entire description provided by the seller. The formal description of the item is located near the middle of the listing page. Usually, a seller goes to great lengths to give you everything you need to know about the item you are bidding on, including who provides the Certificate of Authenticity, shipping costs, taxes (if applicable), and return policy. It's a good idea to read all of this information carefully to make sure you know what you're getting yourself into, as your bid on eBay is regarded as a binding contract. You can't claim ignorance later on if all the facts are spelled out completely in the auction listing. That excuse just won't fly with your seller or with eBay, which most times will ban an irresponsible bidder from using the site after repeated violations of the user agreement.

You also notice that below the item description you usually find a photo (or multiple photos) of the collectible being sold. An experienced seller generally will include a full-size photo of the item, a close-up of the Certificate of

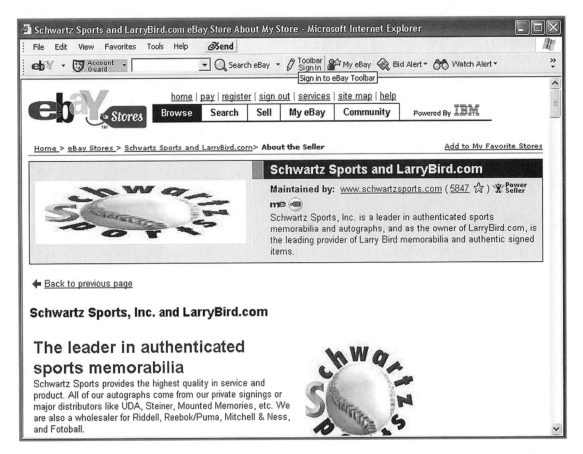

Figure 5.10

The Me page is used for sellers and buyers to provide fellow eBay users more information about themselves, and their companies in many cases. It's a good place to get better acquainted with someone you are contemplating doing business with.

Authenticity or hologram use to authenticate the item, and a separate close-up of the autograph (if the item is signed).

If you do *not* find all the information you want and need before placing a bid on the item, then be advised it is wise to scroll back up to the shaded Seller Information box near the top of the listing. Click the Ask Seller a Question link; up pops a screen that allows you to email a question or concern to this item's seller; see Figure 5.11. An upstanding seller usually answers your question in a matter of minutes or hours, as he is hoping to ease your concerns and convince you to place a bid in his auctions. If you don't get an answer, that typically means the seller either is not monitoring his auctions and correspondence closely enough or perhaps does not want to answer your question. This is a red flag that should warn you: Danger! Avoid this auction! You probably are saving yourself some headaches later on down the line.

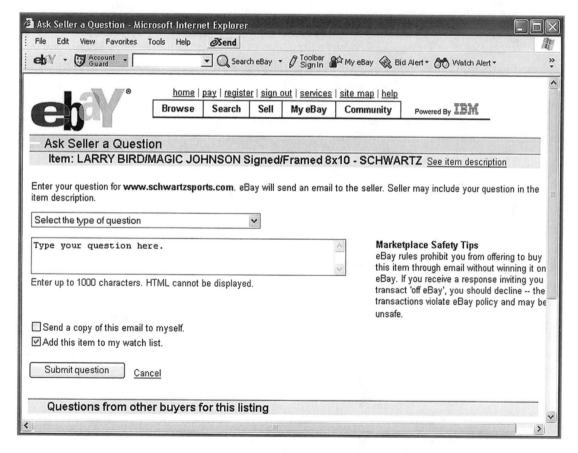

Figure 5.11

This form can be used to ask a seller any questions you might have about an item. The good sellers provide quick responses.

Tip

Save the email correspondence you get from buyers or sellers until no longer needed. If a seller tells you something about your item in an email, and it turns out not to be true, their statement can serve as good evidence against him should you need to file a fraud alert. The same goes for buyers: If a buyer emails you to say he is mailing a payment on a certain day, and that payment never arrives—and never was sent—their email is good evidence that can help lead to an eBay abuser's suspension from trading.

Click the Back button again to return to the original listing. By scrolling down near the bottom of the page, you come across the Payment Methods Accepted information for this item. In this case, the seller accepts PayPal, money orders, Visa/MasterCard, American Express, and Discover credit cards, which you can see in Figure 5.12. Some sellers accept only checks (and there usually is a 10-day to 2-week hold on orders paid by personal check) or money orders. PayPal has become the payment tool of choice on eBay (see Chapter 2, "Pledge Allegiance to eBay"); credit cards usually are accepted only by the bigger eBay sellers, many of whom make their living with auctions.

Ready to Bid?

Just below the Payment Methods area is the area you have been waiting for: the bid area! This is where you type in your bid amount after you decide to try to buy this item. The current high bid is displayed; you are asked for the maximum bid that you wish to place at this time (along with the minimum bid required to just get yourself in the running for the item). For the sake of this exercise, assume you type in a bid of $75.00 and click Place Bid. The next screen, shown in Figure 5.13, reminds you the name of the item you are bidding on, plus the maximum price you have indicated you are willing to pay for it. It also displays your user ID, and if you scroll a bit down the screen, eBay policy on Certificates of Authenticity; see Figure 5.14.

This is a good time to go over eBay's guidelines on a Certificate of Authenticity, which often also is referred to as a COA.

■ **Autograph Buying:** Autographs are commonly sold with a Certificate of Authenticity, also known as a COA. Many COAs come from credible sources, which can add prestige and even financial value to a particular

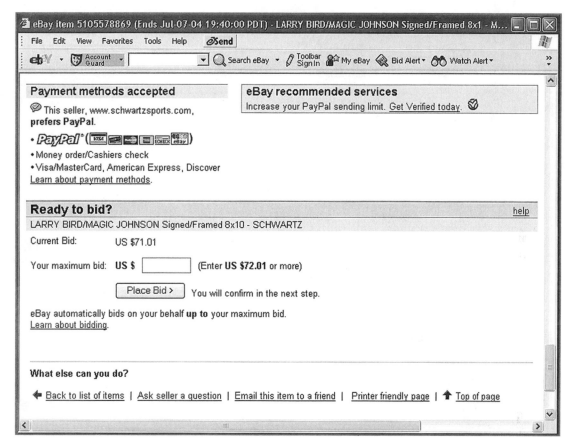

Figure 5.12

Near the bottom of the auction page you find what payment methods are accepted by this seller, along with the box in which to type in your bid.

autograph. Meanwhile, other COAs effectively add no value to an autograph, given that any seller can provide his or her own personal COA—whether the item is authentic or not.

In addressing the potential for fraud, eBay has established certain requirements regarding COAs: If a seller promotes that an item comes with a COA, the seller must provide details about the certificate, including the name of the issuing party. Listings that do not comply with this requirement (see Chapter 4, "Authentication Is Sweeping the Nation")

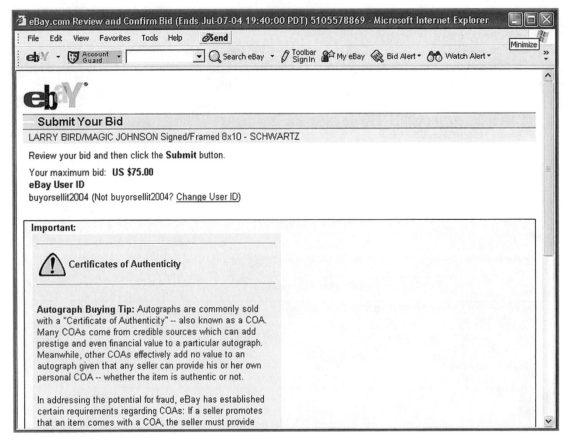

Figure 5.13

This is where you confirm the amount you are willing to bid on this item.

are in violation of eBay policy and may not be covered by eBay's fraud protection service.

- **Get an Expert Opinion:** eBay has sought out qualified experts in the autograph field who, for a nominal fee, evaluate a listing that you wish to bid on and offer their opinion on its authenticity. Trade smart and take advantage of this QuickOpinion service. (See Chapter 4 for more on "QuickOpinion.")

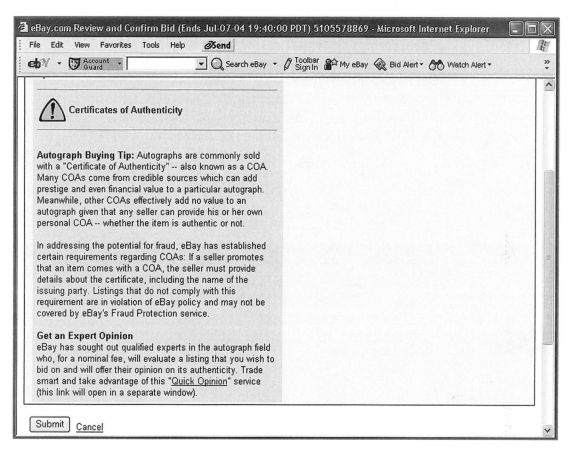

Figure 5.14

You should carefully review eBay's policy on Certificates of Authenticity before bidding.

Here Is the Moment You Have Been Waiting For

You can almost hear the drum roll from the orchestra. Here is the moment you have been waiting for: You have decided how much to bid ($75.00 this case) and you are ready to make your bid official and binding. Scroll down to the very bottom of the page, find the Submit button, and click it . . .

. . . Congratulations! You are the current high bidder!

If your bid was successful, then the next screen that pops up (see Figure 5.15) alerts you that you are the current high bidder. In this exercise, the previous high bidder (at $71.01) has been eclipsed by your bid of $75.00. However, the current high bid is only $72.01 (and not your maximum bid of $75.00). Why is this? Because eBay uses an automatic bidding service for its users. This system is designed to make buying more convenient and less time consuming. You don't need to do anything special to set up your bids this way.

When you bid on an auction-style listing you are placing bids using this method:

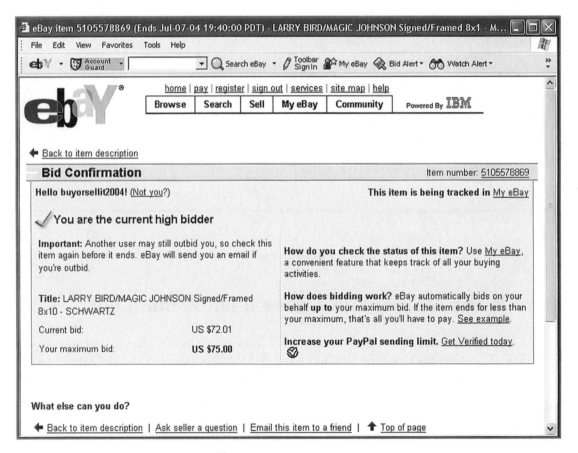

Figure 5.15

This is what you see if your bid is higher than everyone else's so far in the auction process.

1. When you place a bid, you enter the maximum amount you'd be willing to pay for the item. Your maximum amount is kept confidential from other bidders and from the seller.

2. The eBay system compares your bid to those of the other bidders.

3. The system places bids on your behalf, using only as much of your bid as necessary to maintain your high bid position (or to meet the reserve price). The system bids up to your maximum amount.

Note

A reserve price is a tool sellers can use to stimulate bidding on their auction-style item while reserving the right not to sell below a price they have in mind. Many sellers have found that too high a starting price discourages interest in their item, while an attractively low starting price makes them vulnerable to selling at an unsatisfactorily low price. A reserve price helps with this issue.

A seller sets the reserve at the lowest price he is willing to sell the item for. If a bidder does not meet that price, then the seller is not obligated to sell the item. You set your reserve price, as well as a starting price, when you list your item. The reserve price is not disclosed to bidders, but they will be told that your auction has a reserve price and whether or not the reserve has been met.

All reserve price auctions on eBay are subject to a reserve price auction fee that is refunded when the auction is successfully completed. If the item does not sell, this fee is not refunded.

4. If another bidder has a higher maximum, you'll be outbid. If no other bidder has a higher maximum, you win the item. You could pay significantly less than your maximum price! This means you don't have to keep coming back to bid every time another bid is placed.

This bidding system does not apply to multiple item auctions (*Dutch auctions*) and in reserve price auctions. In reserve price auctions, if your maximum bid is the first to be greater than the seller's reserve price, the eBay system automatically jumps the price to meet the reserve and bidding continues from there.

Note

When you see a quantity of two or more in an eBay auction, that is referred to as a "Dutch" auction. This means the seller is offering multiple, identical items for sale. Unlike a regular eBay auction, multiple item auctions can have many winners.

When you bid on a multiple item auction, you specify the number of items you're interested in and the price you're willing to pay. All winning bidders will pay the same price: the lowest successful bid.

Much of the time, all buyers pay the starting price in multiple item auctions. However, if there are more bids than items, the items will go to the earliest successful bids. To beat another bid, yours must have a higher total bid per item than other bids, regardless of how many items you are bidding on. Reducing this total bid value in subsequent bids is not permitted.

What if I Change My Mind?

What is the best thing to do if you're not sure whether to bid or are unsure how much to bid? Not bid at all. If you type in a bid amount and arrive at the screen where you are asked to submit your bid, you have the option of canceling your bid. You can click the Cancel button (refer to Figure 5.14) if you are not completely certain you want to bid this amount in this auction.

What is eBay's policy on bidding? Simple: You bid on it, you buy it (assuming you are the high bidder). Place a bid only if you're serious about buying the item. If you are the winning bidder, you enter into a legally binding contract to purchase the item from the seller. If have any questions about the item you are bidding on, get those questions answered before you do any bidding.

What if you mistakenly entered $7500.00 instead of $75.00 when you made your original bid? Don't fret, as there is a way to fix the problem. On the eBay site map, under Buyer Tools, there is a link to the page that helps you retract your bid. There, eBay reminds you that you should read the item description very carefully and check out the seller's feedback before making a bid. You are reminded to ask the seller any and all questions before making a bid. eBay reminds you that every bid is binding (unless the item is listed in a category under the non-binding bid policy or the transaction is prohibited by law or by eBay's user agreement). eBay also reminds you that bidding on multiple identical items (for instance, bidding on the same exact item being sold by multiple but different sellers) should be done only if you intend to purchase all of the items. Bidding on the same item from multiple sellers and then retracting your bids after you win one of the items is enough to get you thrown off the site!

When can you retract a bid on eBay?

- If you mistakenly enter a wrong bid amount (for example, you bid $7500.00 instead of $75.00). If this happens, eBay requests that you go back to the item and reenter the correct bid amount immediately.

- If the description of the item you are bidding on changes significantly.

- If you are unable to contact the seller before the auction ends. This means that you have tried calling the seller and the seller's phone number doesn't work, or you have tried emailing the seller and it comes back undeliverable.

Once you have successfully placed a bid on eBay, you receive an email saying so. The notice is delivered to the email address that you provided during your registration process. See Figure 5.16. This is why it's a good idea to check off that little box allowing emails generated by eBay when you complete the registration process—you want to know when you bid, win, list, or sell an item, right?

What if I Get Outbid?

Even though your bid of $75.00 originally might have made you the high bidder at one time, that doesn't necessarily mean you will win the auction. Remember, there are millions of other eBay users out there, and several hundreds (or thousands) of them might just be looking for an item similar to yours. You might get outbid a few minutes later, a couple hours later, or just before the auction ends. That's why it is advisable to enter a maximum bid so that the proxy bidding system bids up to the highest amount you feel comfortable with.

How do you know if you have been outbid? If another buyer places a higher bid than yours, eBay sends an email to the address you provided during registration (see Figure 5.17). Inside of that email is a link that that should take you

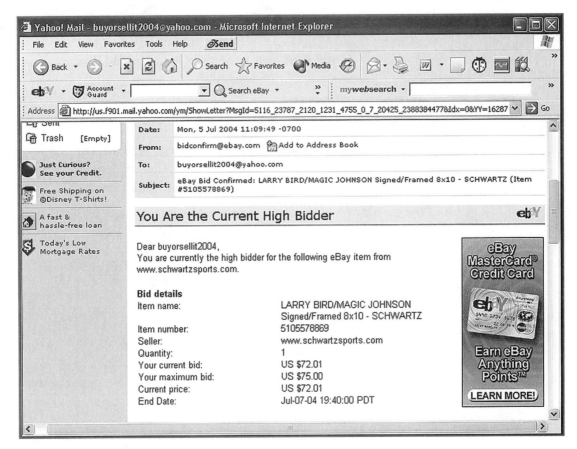

Figure 5.16

eBay notifies you by email if you are the current high bidder.

directly to the item's auction page. If you decide it's worth putting in another, higher bid, this is a simple way to place an increased amount on file for the proxy bidding process. If not, simply delete the email and move on to other auctions.

How Do I Monitor My Bids?

Once you have bid on one or more auctions, keeping track of them is quite simple, thanks to the eBay search engine. You can even bookmark the items you are bidding on and occasionally check back to see where you stand with

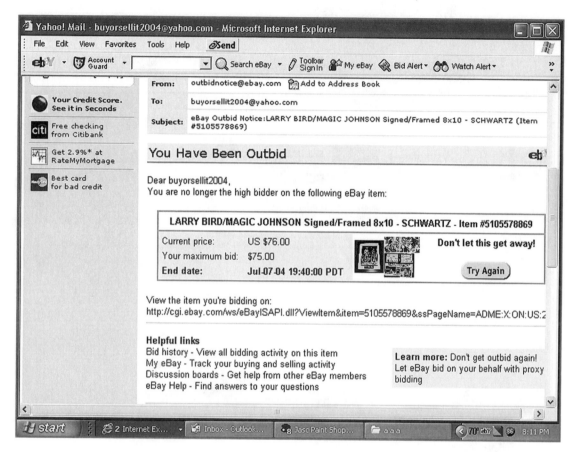

Figure 5.17

eBay notifies you by email if are outbid. The email provides a link for you to place another bid, should you decide to stay in the running.

them. This is particularly useful should you get outbid on an item. By creating a bookmark for the items you have bid on, you can just use that to create a quasi-checklist of items that you are interested in.

To create this bookmark, follow these steps:

1. Click Search at the top of any eBay page.

2. Click the By Bidder tab shown in Figure 5.18.

3. Type in your eBay user ID and click Search.

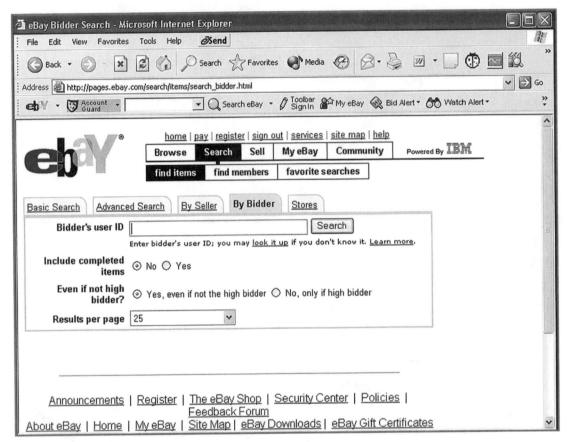

Figure 5.18

Click the Search button; then click By Bidder.

What is displayed is a current list of items that you have bids on (see Figure 5.19), listed according to end date and time. The list displays the item number, auction start and end times and dates, current price, auction title, the name of the high bidder, and the name of the seller.

This list helps you monitor your inventory of items as you become more and more accustomed to using eBay, and thus feel increasingly comfortable about placing more and more bids. Pretty soon you have dozens, if not more, auc-

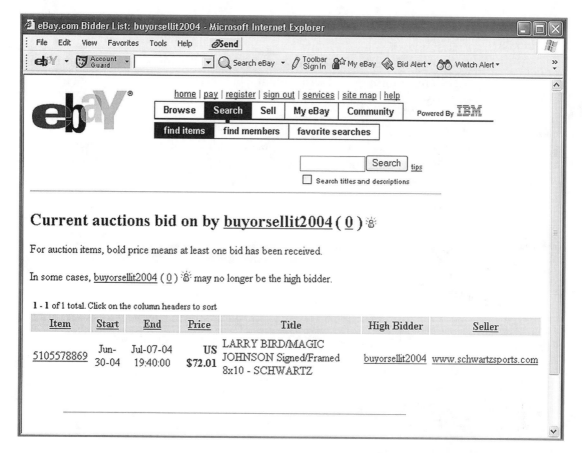

Figure 5.19

Example of a search list of auctions you have bid on.

tions that you are bidding in at the same time. At that point, it not only is about auction management: It can be about money management, too!

The bidder search can be customized to display items this way:

- Items on which you have placed high bids over the past 30 days

- All the items you have bid on over the past 30 days, whether you are the current high bidder or have won the auction

Getting to Know My eBay

Another useful eBay function to get acquainted with would be the My eBay page. This information is easily obtainable by clicking the My eBay tab on the top of any eBay page; see Figure 5.20.

By scrolling up and down the My eBay page, the tabs for monitoring your auctions are easily accessible. You can sort to pull up information on items you are bidding on, items you've won, items you have added to a watch list, and items that you did not win. There also are several category searches for sellers as well as links to other things:

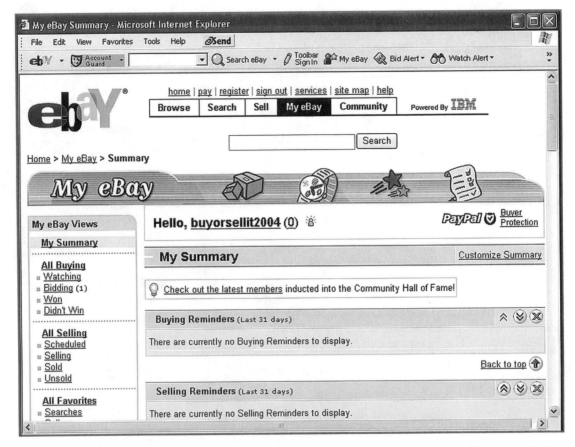

Figure 5.20

By clicking My eBay, you can check on pretty much all your eBay activity in one spot.

■ Your eBay account page, which keeps track of funds you may owe eBay as a seller

■ Your PayPal account

■ Dispute resolution (see Chapter 4)

■ eBay announcements regarding site improvements and updates

You can save favorite categories, searches, sellers, and stores to quickly and easily find what you want. You can also sign up for email alerts so you know immediately when new items that meet your collecting interests are listed for sale. These lists can be customized to display results from over the past 24 hours to the past 60 days.

You can also view your account status, manage your seller account, and pay your seller fees via the My eBay page.

eBay Toolbar

Another helpful tool provided free of charge is the eBay toolbar, which can be added to your desktop. The eBay toolbar, shown in Figure 5.21, allows for quick access to the eBay web site, tracks the items you have bid on, tracks auctions you are watching, and alerts you before those auctions end so you can place a bid if you'd like. It could mean the difference between forgetting to bid and winning the auction!

The eBay toolbar also comes with Account Guard, a new feature that helps you protect your eBay account information. Account Guard warns you when you are on a potentially fraudulent (spoof) web site—those that try to look and act like eBay, but really aren't. It also lets you report such sites to eBay. Account Guard is only available for Microsoft Internet Explorer.

Look Out! There's a Sniper!

So far I have only discussed browsing through eBay auctions using the search engine. A good many eBay users prefer to monitor auctions and put their bids in at the very last possible second, hoping to steal an item from another collector. Be advised, however, that sometimes this works out quite well while

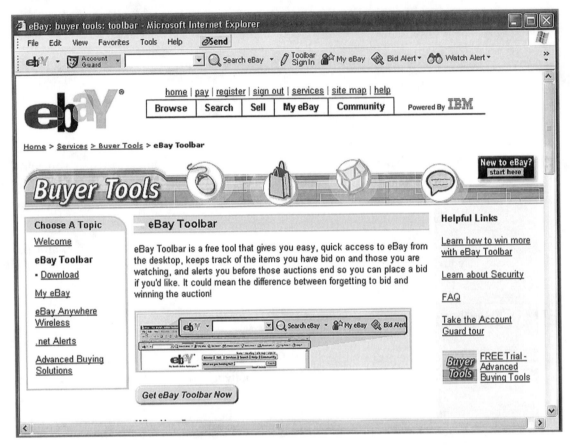

Figure 5.21

The eBay toolbar can be added right to your desktop for quick, easy access to eBay.

other times it can lead to extreme disappointment. You can quickly go from the thrill of victory to the agony of defeat.

This process, called sniping, as well as ill-timed yet unavoidable computer or network problems, can prevent you from putting in that last-second bid you hoped would do the trick. You might be all ready to click in a last-second bid at what you think is a winning price, only to be thwarted by your laptop's tardy response. It can and does happen, with your item subsequently being sold to another buyer who actually bid less than what your ceiling bid might have been. Arrghh!

If you found an auction that might interest you, there is an Add to Watch List link near the top-right side of the page (see Figure 5.22). By clicking this link, eBay automatically adds this item to your personal watch list. That list can be viewed by clicking My eBay, then clicking the watch list sort on the left side of the page (see Figure 5.23). You can always delete any items you want from your watch list with a simple click of the mouse.

If you get outbid at the last minute on an item you desperately hoped to win, don't get too down. It happens all the time and will happen again—to you and to everyone else who braves the eBay world. That is why last-minute bidding and settling only for bargain prices sometimes do not pay off.

Figure 5.22

You can monitor the bidding on selected eBay auctions by clicking the Add to Watch List button.

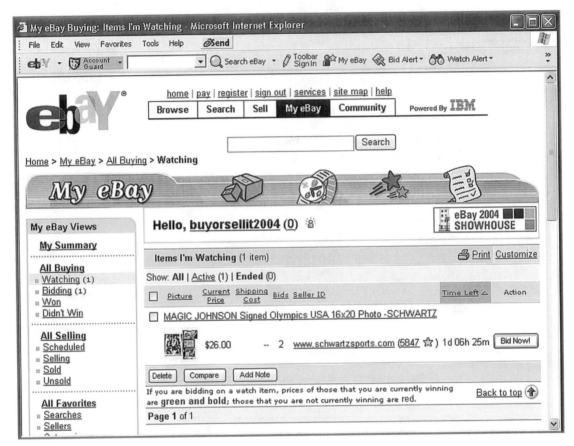

Figure 5.23

The auctions you are monitoring are displayed by the items you are watching on eBay.

The process of last-minute bidding is referred to as sniping, which means placing a high bid in the closing seconds of an auction-style listing. To some, this sniping process might seem unfair, but to others it is a way of life, and in reality it is just part of the eBay experience. The highest bid wins the auction, no matter when the bid was placed.

One way to help avoid disappointment is to ensure that the maximum bid you enter is the highest price that you're willing to pay. The eBay proxy system automatically increases your bid up to the maximum price you specify, so entering a higher maximum may help prevent you from being outbid in the closing seconds of a listing. There also are several well-documented computer programs that some eBay users employ to help improve their sniping skills, many of which can be purchased right on eBay itself.

Don't Mix E-Commerce with E-motions

Everyone knows it's a bad idea to stay out in the sun too long. Same goes for doing business with family or friends. Usually, you are just asking for trouble.

Same goes for mixing the e-commerce of eBay with the emotions you might have as a collector. If you let your emotions get in the way of your bidding, don't be surprised if you wind up paying too much for an item. Sometimes pride and greed can get in the way, and the "I just have to have it" approach can't be overcome. Unless it's a rare find, a one-of-a-kind item (such as a 1927 Yankees team-signed baseball), or something that you're completely certain you'll never see again, you're probably better off setting up some bidding parameters for yourself before you get in too deep. Here are a few questions to consider answering as you prepare to do business:

- How much am I willing to spend?
- How soon do I need this item?
- Can I wait for the "best" deal?
- Will this item come along again soon?
- Does condition matter?
- How much is shipping?
- What is the seller's feedback?

Remember, too, bidding too high and retracting can come back to haunt you. Sellers are notified by eBay via email when bids are retracted on their auctions. A retracted bid can stir the anger of any eBay seller who is offering a high-priced item; a retracted bid obviously can adversely affect the closing price on his auction. If a bid is retracted in the last few hours before an auction is scheduled to end, who knows how many bidders who earlier had passed on bidding in that auction will go back to see what the current price is? There is just no way of telling. There are more than just a few eBay sellers who will block you from bidding in their auctions if they see you have retracted more than one or two bids over the past few days or weeks (especially in their auctions).

Many sellers make their living by selling on eBay, and sometimes blocking a troublesome bidder is the only way these sellers can keep the playing field level for themselves and for the buyers who are out there placing serious bids. So retracting a bid should only be done in the most serious of circumstances.

part 3

Selling Sports Collectibles
on eBay

chapter 6

Getting Ready to Sell

Not long ago it all seemed like just one big joke to many folks. If somebody famous in the entertainment world had a tooth removed, the late-night pundits often were quick to jump on the news and fire out a punch line: ". . . and it'll be on sale tomorrow morning on eBay," was sometimes how they would put it. The studio audience would giggle with glee.

But selling on eBay is no longer such a laughing matter. Instead, it has become the "in" thing in many circles, and now some people won't think you're "with it" unless you have a stable of auctions going. "You mean you *don't* sell on eBay?" is the way the conversation might evolve. Putting baseball cards, autographed photos, or game-used bats up for sale has become a way of life for some, and for many others it has become a serious way of making a living. Hundreds and hundreds of people have given up their day jobs and now—instead of being laughed at—are laughing all the way to the bank with the money they make on eBay.

It's not hard to sell someone on the lifestyle. Where else can you report to work in your bathrobe, or your swimsuit, or even in your *birthday suit* if you so desire? Where else can you set your own work hours, set your own work days, or just not report to work at all if you just don't feel like it on any given day? All of this and more are possible by selling on eBay.

Your boss wants you to work overtime? If your business is based on eBay, only *you* can tell yourself *when* and *if* you can go on vacation! Indeed, selling on eBay is a manner of making money that suits pretty much everyone's needs, hopes, lifestyles, and dreams. There has been a population boom of small-business owners thanks to eBay—an explosion of entrepreneurs who auction off merchandise by just using a computer located in their home, garage, or basement.

Selling on eBay obviously is fun, or else there wouldn't be the throng of folks who swear by it. Make no mistake—it also is hard work. You have to be driven, you have to have initiative, and have to be a self-starter, and you have to be accountable to yourself. You have nobody else to blame if the income is not coming in—that's because you look the boss in the mirror every morning.

This is not to say that only full-time sellers use and profit from eBay. It's quite the contrary. Many folks are just looking for a hobby and find that buying and selling on eBay is not only fun, but a learning experience, too. Other folks use eBay as a part-time job to help supplement their income. Others just want to experience the thrill and excitement (seriously) that only comes from bidding in a live auction.

It can be fun and exciting for full-time sellers, too. I can remember the first time I listed an item for sale on eBay. I had no idea if my item would actually sell, but I decided to just give it my best shot. I checked the listing two or three times a day during the course of the seven-day auction, just to see if somebody out there actually would buy something from me. When the bids began coming in, I wanted to keep tabs on the auction even more. Then, on the very last day, I was almost glued to my computer screen, watching the minutes and seconds tick down as the end of auction drew near. I repeatedly refreshed my screen—it must have been 20 or 30 times—during the final minute to check and see if the price would go up. Whew! When it ended and *somebody actually bought my item,* it brought a rush of adrenaline I'd never expected! I definitely was hooked.

I had actually sold an item on eBay! I was almost giddy. Somebody actually decided to take a chance on an eBay newbie (me) and send some real, hard cash (theirs) for a previously owned item (mine). Kind of neat, actually.

Well, if you've never auctioned off an item before, you're in for a treat. I will take you through the listing process, step by step, and try to help you avoid some of the pitfalls that first-time sellers often experience. I'll try to make it as easy and simple as possible. Hopefully, you'll remember (and reuse later on) some of the tips and shortcuts that might bring you more and bigger bids for the items you are selling. But as I've often stressed before on previous pages of the book, it's only with hard work that you will become a success. Remember to do your homework!

Are you ready to get started?

Let's Make a Deal

Okay, so you've got an item you think somebody else is just itching to own. Are you ready to sell?

For the sake of this exercise, let's say you want to auction off a baseball autographed by Barry Bonds. From the eBay home page (www.ebay.com), locate

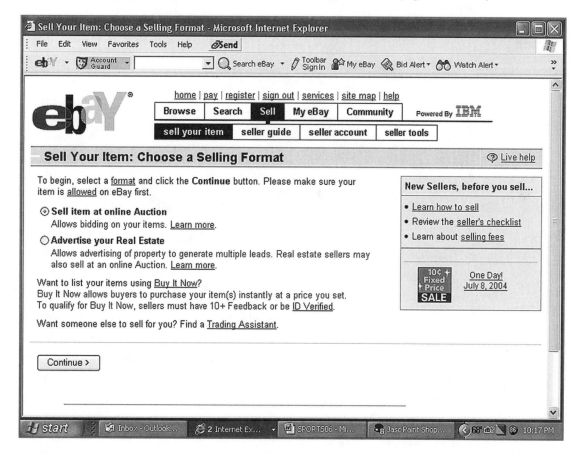

Figure 6.1

From the eBay home page, if you click on Sell, you should next choose the online Auction format.

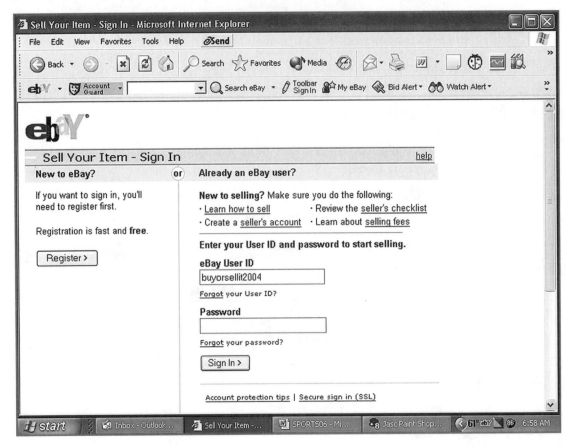

Figure 6.2

You will need to log in with your eBay user ID and password to begin the listing process.

and click on the Sell button at the top of the page. That will position you with your first decision as a seller (see Figure 6.1). You have the option of selling your item through the online Auction format, or as part of eBay's Real Estate listings. And while some might joke you can pay your monthly mortgage with the money you might spend on a Bonds autographed baseball, you'll obviously want to pick the online Auction format here.

The next screen that pops up on your computer (see Figure 6.2) will prompt you to enter your eBay user ID along with your password. Type in your user ID and password, click the Sign In button, and you're on your way!

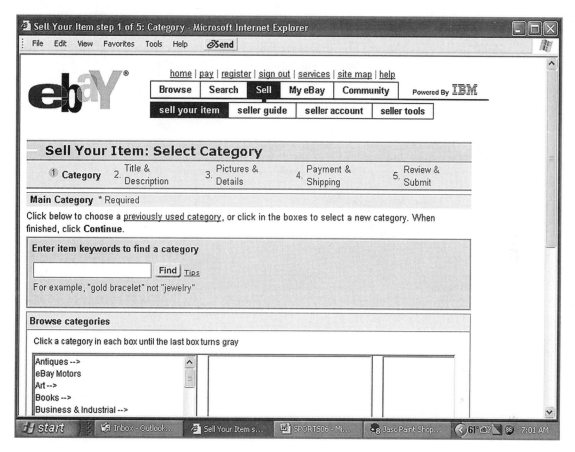

Figure 6.3

You will need to select in which category to list your item.

Your next decision will be to choose what category (see Figure 6.3) to list your item in. In this case, click into the Browse Categories area and select Sports Mem, Cards & Fan Shop (see Figure 6.4). This will allow you to take the next step (see Figure 6.5) of clicking on Memorabilia in the second box on this screen.

Your next choice would be to highlight Autographs-Original in the following box (see Figure 6.6). This all might seem tedious at first, but you want to make a sale and get the best price possible, right? It will be worth it later on, so don't give up now!

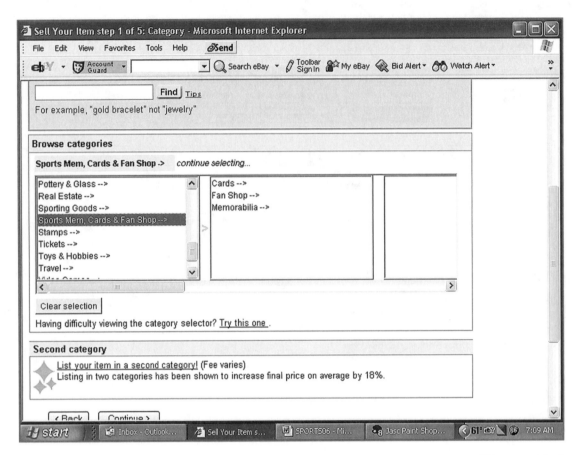

Figure 6.4

For this exercise, you are using the Sports Mem, Cards & Fan Shop category.

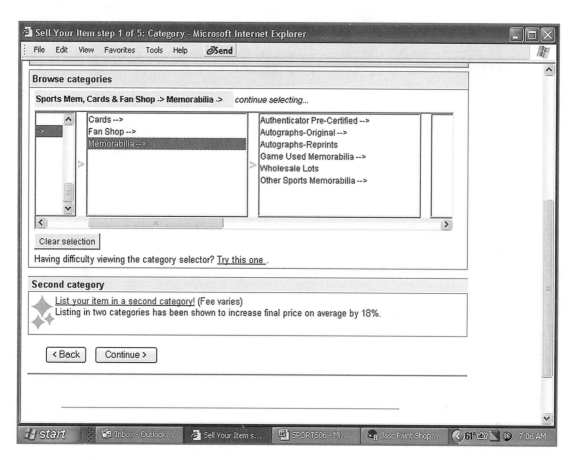

Figure 6.5

Use the Memorabilia category listing on the drop-down menu.

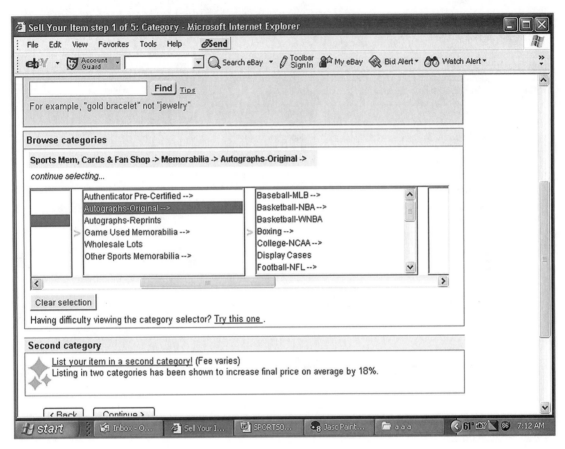

Figure 6.6

Next, use the Autographs-Original category listing.

Next, go ahead and select Baseball-MLB (see Figure 6.7), and finally select Balls (see Figure 6.8).

At this point, eBay will inform you that you have your "Main category selected / Continue below" in the last display box that is on your screen. This box is slightly tinted to let you know that no further category selection is needed. Your next step is to click on the Continue button at the bottom of the page. That will bring up the next screen.

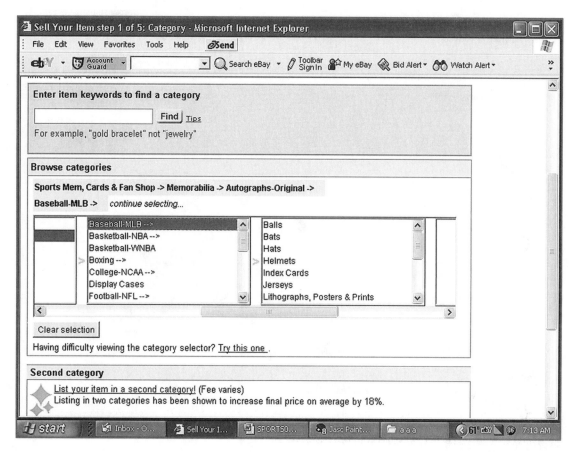

Figure 6.7

For this listing you will use the Baseball-MLB category.

Now comes the real selling part. The next screen you see (see Figure 6.9) will ask you to describe your item. Type in the item title. Decide whether it is appropriate to use the Subtitle area. For just 50 cents, the Subtitle area is a bargain since it allows you to provide prospective buyers with even more information about your item. You will notice that the Item title area allows you to type in only 55 characters and that no quotes, asterisks, or HTML are allowed. In this case, I typed in "Barry Bonds Autographed Baseball" as the title of the auction.

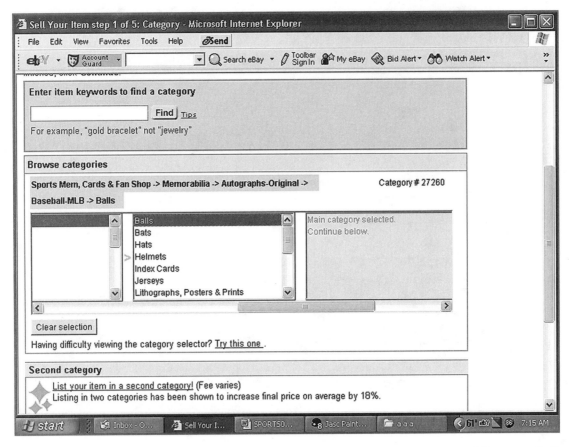

Figure 6.8

The final choice for this category listing is Balls.

How to Write a Good Description

Here are some tips on writing a good title description:

- Use words that clearly describe what you are selling. Buyers will be searching eBay by keywords to find items such as yours, so abbreviations usually don't work.

- Use as much of the allotted 55-character space as possible. You are paying for this real estate, so use it wisely.

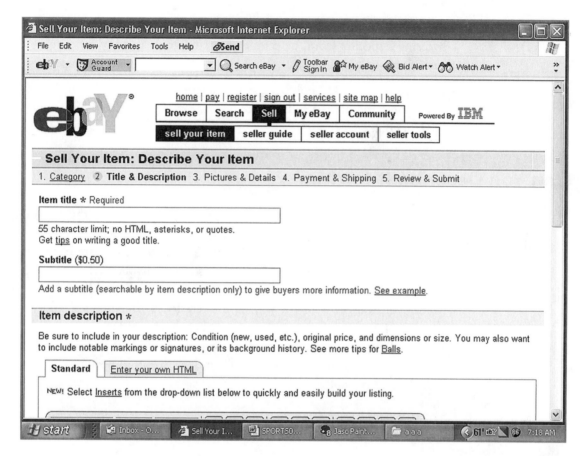

Figure 6.9

In this area, you will be able to choose an item title and subtitle for your auction.

- Be sure to include your item's brand name or athlete's name as it applies. If you are selling a Magic Johnson item, you will get more hits on your item if you use the word "Magic" with your listing, and not just describe it as "Johnson autograph ball."

- If your item includes authentication by one of the major memorabilia or card companies (Steiner, Upper Deck, Fleer, Topps, etc.), be sure to include that in your description as well.

- State exactly what your item is, even if that means repeating the category name (ball or photo, for instance).

■ If you think a prospective buyer will be searching for an item like yours by using a specific word, be certain to include that and any other relevant words or terms.

■ Do your homework! Look back at past auction listings to see which titles closed the highest bids. There is a reason we all studied history in grade school.

Can You Describe It for Me?

The next step is writing a larger-scale description of your item in the auction listing form. The eBay auction listing form (see Figure 6.10) allows you to type in as much information as you think necessary. Remember, you are trying to persuade a potential buyer into bidding for this item, so you need to offer up as much information as you know about it. Put yourself in the bidder's place—what would you want to know if you were interested in this item? If a lot of crucial information is left out, you can almost bet that potential buyers will be emailing or calling you to ask questions or worse: They might just decide not to bid at all. A bad description can cost you money, so it's important to do as thorough a job as possible.

How Does That Look?

One of the really neat, easy-to-use tools that eBay provides for sellers is the ability to code your description using different fonts, colors, and point sizes. This can really make your listing look professional and draw more interest from potential buyers. For example, your item description can just be in regular type, in paragraph form like you see Figure 6.11. However, if you opt to use some of the eBay text enhancements, it can really liven up your listing; see Figure 6.12. Which one do you think will draw more interest? The best advice is to play around with the different fonts, colors, and point sizes until you find a format that works for you. Define a portion of the text after you have it typed in, select a different font, point size, and color, and then see how it looks. It's just a matter of taste, according to each individual seller.

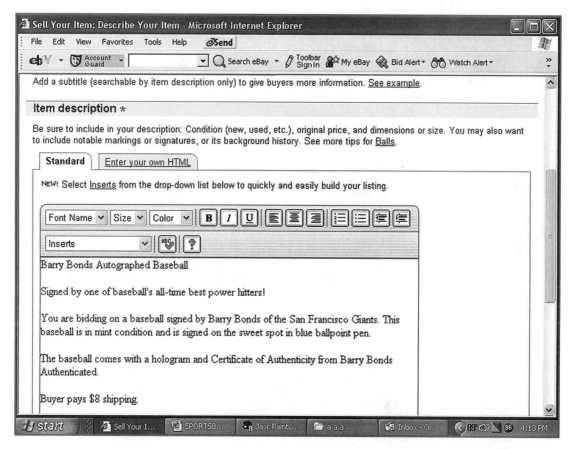

Figure 6.10

The item description area allows you to use as much, or as little, text as you need to describe your auction.

Some sellers like to use dozens of different pieces of information in their listings. I prefer to make the description attractive, yet short, punchy, and informative. Remember, most people browsing through the thousands of items on eBay only have a limited amount of time to look at your listing, so make it eye-catching. Be sincere, offer as much pertinent information as possible, and remember that when you write the description to put yourself in the buyer's place: What would you want to know about your item if you were the prospective bidder?

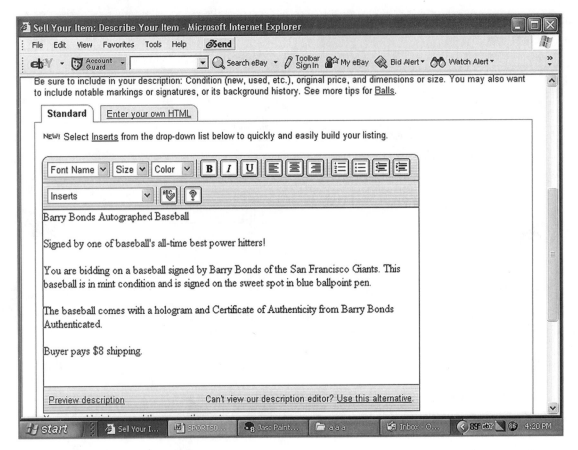

Figure 6.11

If you so choose, you can leave your description displayed in regular text, such as this.

You will be able to add photos to enhance your auction on the next page of the listing process, so once you are satisfied with your item description, click on Continue.

Details, Details

Your next task will be to add photos and additional information about your item as necessary. You will notice that the item title and subtitle are already in place on the page shown in Figure 6.12.

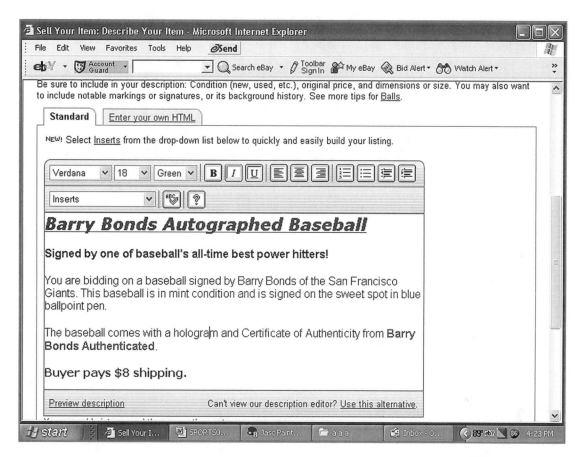

Figure 6.12

By using the eBay tools, you can change the appearance of the type in the description. This can help bring attention to your item and bring more bids.

Next, you need to decide what price you would like to start your auction at (see Figure 6.13). The starting price is what the bidding will begin at. Most sellers have found that setting the starting price too high will discourage bidding, so you need to keep this in mind. Remember, if you've ever seen a live auction—in person, on television, in the movies, or whatever—you know that the bidding always starts with a relatively low figure. Then, if it's an item many folks are excited about owning, the pace of the bidding often can take on a life of its own, ending with a last-second frenzy that means more dollars in your pocket. But remember, the starting price also could be the price that

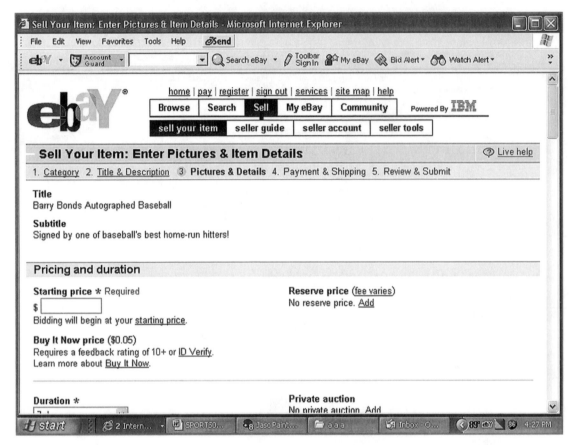

Figure 6.13

What is the starting price you'd like to begin your auction at?

your auction ends at (if there is only one bid, for example), unless you decide to specify a reserve price.

If you are using the fixed-price format, then you'll need to enter a Buy It Now price that you will accept from any buyer who is willing to pay that amount. Simply enter the price at which you wish to sell your item. Then, if a bidder comes along and sees your item and is willing to pay your Buy It Now price, the bidding thus would end with just one bid. Usually, however, the thrill of the chase is what entices many people to bid in an auction.

When to Use a Reserve Price

This is a tricky question to answer. If you decide to add a reserve price (see Chapter 5, "Getting Ready to Bid") to your listing, then you run the risk of not selling your item at all, should no buyers enter a bid equal to or surpassing your reserve. Then, you've got to relist the item all over again, and perhaps repeat the very same process a third, fourth, or fifth time with the same item until you either get the price you wanted or just give up selling the item at all. If you're sensing that I've had frustration with reserve auctions, you are correct.

Here is the fine line: If you do not set a reserve price, then your item will be sold to the highest bidder, no matter where the bidding winds up. If you have an item that has sold for $200 the past few times it has appeared on eBay, then most savvy bidders probably already know that already and will perhaps bid up to that price, but maybe no higher. However, it is impossible to predict exactly what every bidder out there is thinking. And it is impossible to know whether another buyer is going to come along and pay that same $200 for your item, even though the same item sold for $200 on several different occasions over the past 30 days.

The flip side of this: If a buyer has not done his homework, is new to collecting, or just *really needs* your item as soon as possible, it is not unheard of for the same item to sell for substantially more than past auctions. That is why the auction world is so fascinating and exciting to so many buyers and sellers alike—you never really know what's going to happen until it does. There is no predicting the future.

How Long Should I Run My Auction?

This is another question difficult to answer. Some sellers always use seven-day auctions. Others prefer three days. Still others are convinced that weekends are the best days to end an auction, since buyers will be at home and off work on Saturdays and Sundays. There also is a group of sellers who firmly believe that ending an auction on a weekend, when many people want to get away from their computers, is not such a good idea; these sellers often end their auctions in the evenings on weekdays. Still others maintain that not everybody has access to a computer at home, so it is better to end your auctions on weekdays when more office workers can sneak a peak at your listings on their lunch hours or while the boss isn't looking.

The bottom line is this: *You* have to decide how long you want to run your auction listing. Your built-in choices from eBay are 1 day, 3 days, 5 days, 7 days, or 10 days (the latter of which will cost you an extra 20 cents per listing). Once you also have decided when you would like your auction to end (this takes a bit of looking at the calendar or your crystal ball), then subtract the time period you choose to run your auction (seven days, five days, three days, etc.) and begin your auction at that date and time.

One of the best pieces of advice I can offer regarding selling sports memorabilia is to time your auctions around what you see as your buyers' interests. If the Super Bowl is coming up next Sunday, then it might be a good idea to end your auctions on Saturday or Monday. I can guarantee you that most of the world will be in front of their television sets, probably not their computers, all day long on Super Sunday. If you end your auction that day, you are looking for a big letdown.

The same approach applies to personal achievement by an athlete. When Barry Bonds closed in on the 600 home-run club, auction prices on his items climbed in concert. And when he finally did hit number 600, Bonds was in the news so much on television, radio, newspapers, and magazines, the prices on Bonds autographed baseballs hit what was then an all-time high. That said, it is recommended that being a sports fan and carefully following the news is extremely important if you want to sell sports memorabilia. In this business, timing can be everything!

You also can decide to begin your auction when your information is submitted or to pay an additional 10 cents to choose a later date and time to begin the sale. This feature is particularly helpful should you have time to work on your listings, say, on a weekend but you'd prefer to have your auctions actually start on Monday morning (or on another day during the week). This way, that strategy is possible to implement, even though you might not be able to do the work on your computer Monday morning.

For the purposes of this example, let's assume you have one Barry Bonds signed baseball to sell, have chosen to begin the bidding at $1.00, and decided that the auction will run for a period of 10 days; see Figure 6.14. You also will choose a future date and time for the auction to begin.

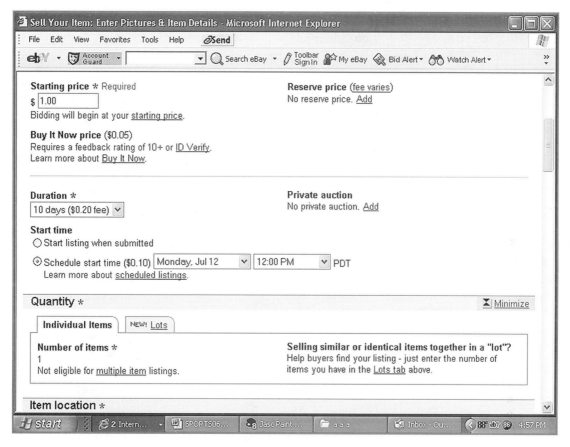

Figure 6.14

eBay gives you the option of running your auction for 1, 3, 5, 7, or 10 days.

The item location has already defaulted to the city and state that accompanied your registration information, but eBay allows you to switch that information if needed by clicking on the Change link that also is found on this page.

You Ought to Be in Pictures

Words and description are crucial to a good auction listing. But perhaps there is nothing more important to convincing buyers to bid in your auctions than photographs—and nice photos, at that. Depending on how much auctioning you plan to do, it's probably a good idea to invest in a digital camera to facilitate inputting photos of your items quickly and easily into your computer so those images can be used in your eBay auctions.

When I first started out selling on eBay, I would take photographs of my auction items with a regular film camera, pay to get the film developed and pay even more for prints, and then scan the photos into my computer. That is a long, tedious process, and you never know how your photos will turn out until you get the prints back. But with a digital camera, you can snap several photos of your items, see how they look in the digital display, and then immediately download them into your computer in a matter minutes. It cuts down the process immensely from what previously took hours or days to accomplish.

How many photos do you want to run with your auction? That's easy . . . as many as possible to help sell your item for the best price possible! If you are selling a ballpark program from the 1961 World Series, you'll probably get a lot of bids anyway, despite whatever words you use in your description. But if you include some nice photos of this vintage item, including the cover and maybe even the roster pages from inside the publication, the odds are you will realize a much higher final selling price than if you went without more detail. If a picture of Mickey Mantle (one of the icons of the sports-collecting marketplace) happens to be in one of your photos, that is almost guaranteed to increase the selling price of your item.

Seeing is believing. The more that potential buyers can see of your item (including photos that indicate the condition of the item), the more likely you will receive more and bigger bids.

Now let's get to adding photos in your auction listing. Scroll down this page a bit further and you will come across the section called eBay Picture Services (see Figure 6.15). If you have access to your own web publishing for your photos, then you can input the address of your photos in this section. However, eBay offers you a chance to have it host your photos online and at minimal cost.

By clicking on one of the spots that says Add Pictures, a selection box linking to images on your computer will pop up on your screen. By selecting the proper photo and then clicking on Add, that photo will be linked to your eBay listing form (see Figure 6.16). Again, for the purposes of this example, let's assume that is the only photo you have to use with this listing.

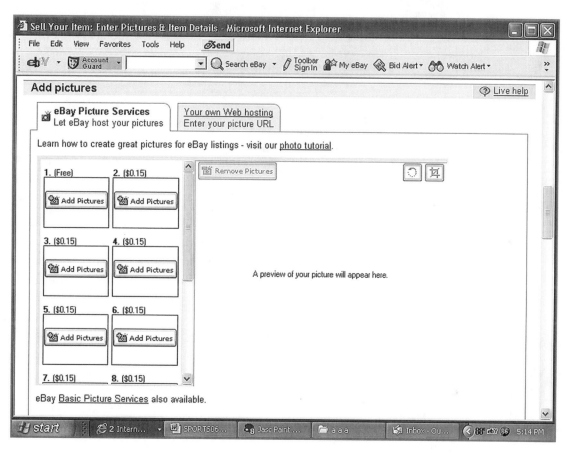

Figure 6.15

You can use this section to upload photos that will be included with your auction.

By scrolling down a bit further on this same screen, you will see that eBay offers you the option of using your photo at standard measure (which will make them appear in a 400×300-pixel area on the listing).

■ For an additional 75 cents, you have the option of allowing potential buyers to click on your image and see it in an enlarged version (500×375 pixels), which is advantageous if you are selling, say, a framed 16×20 photograph. Buyers will be able to see a larger image with much more detail in this version.

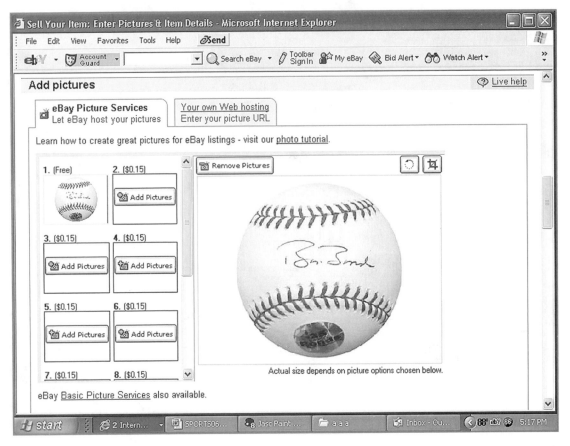

Figure 6.16

The photos you choose to upload will appear in the boxes on this page.

- For another 75 cents, you can choose to show your item using several different photographs in a slide show presentation.

- For another $1.00 you can combine the display of six different photos with the ability to allow buyers to enlarge your image and place your main image in the eBay Gallery.

- For another $1.50 you can have 7 to 12 photos plus Gallery access and the ability to enlarge.

If you have a lot of photos to show your buyers, the final two options sometimes can prove beneficial and cost-effective.

There are two other nice features offered by eBay to help make your listing look professional. The first is the Listing Designer that you see Figure 6.17, in which you can select a theme and a layout to complement your listing. The second pertains to increasing the visibility of your auction among buyers. You have the option to pay additional money for these options to make your listing stand out from the rest:

■ 25 cents to appear in the eBay Gallery. This option is recommended.

■ 25 cents to have a gift icon added to your listing. Helps buyers quickly scope out and identify items that might make for good gifts.

■ $1 for bold (which adds instant emphasis to your listing).

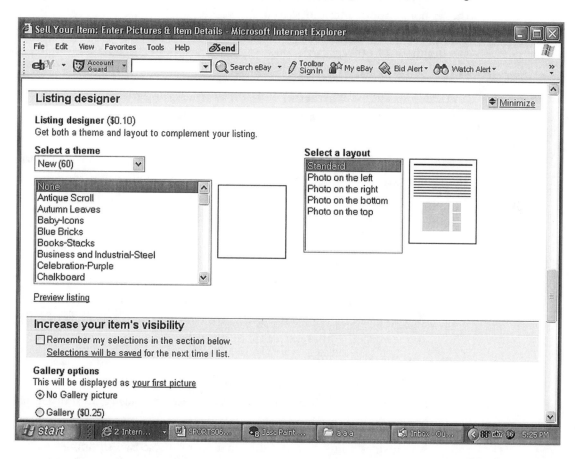

Figure 6.17

The Listing Designer allows you to spice up the appearance of your auction if desired.

- $3 for a border. (surrounds your listing with a border to showcase it)

- $5 to have it highlighted. (highlights your item with a colored band for added emphasis)

- $19.95 or $39.95 to appear in the Featured Plus! or Home Page Featured categories. Recommended for rare, high-priced items you wish to have get as much exposure as possible.

Any of these is helpful if you are willing to pay for them, but not recommended for items that will sell in the $1–$25 price range. Fact is, the more gadgets you use to make your auction stand out, the better. However, what you do must be cost-effective. If you are selling a $2 trading card, it would be senseless to use the $1 bold option, and idiotic to use the $5 highlight option. However, if you are selling a $200 signed jersey, and you want your auction to stand out from the hundreds of other jerseys being sold that day, both the bold and highlight options might be a good deal.

You can also choose whether or not you want a counter on your auctions to substantiate how many eBay users have clicked onto to your item listing to check it out.

Again, for the sake of this exercise, let's pretend you choose to list your item in the Gallery and to boldface the listing to attract more attention from buyers (see Figure 6.18). Next, click on Continue and the eBay Picture System will upload your photographs, bringing up a new screen.

Don't Get Carried Away on a Ship

Now, you will be asked to enter your payment and shipping information (see Figure 6.19). You can tell your buyers that you accept payment by PayPal, check, money order, and credit cards (if you have a merchant account with a bank to accept credit cards).

You also can choose whether to list a flat shipping fee for your bidders or whether your item will be shipped by the U.S. Postal Service (USPS) or United Parcel Service (UPS).

eBay also provides a link to more information for these two shipping services, in addition to a Freight Resource Center if your item is bulky and weighs 150 pounds or more. But what service you choose should depend on what kind of

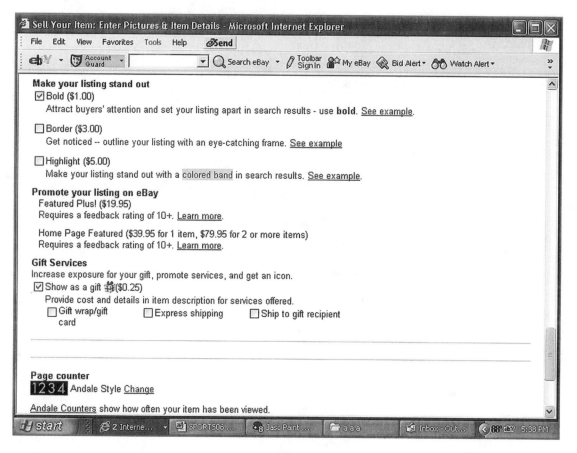

Figure 6.18

By using the boldface option, you can bring more attention to your listing on eBay since several other buyers may have the same item as you.

item you are selling. If you are selling a sports card, it's best probably to use USPS (either First Class or Priority Mail, which offers delivery confirmation); insurance also is recommended if the item is worth a lot of money. For larger items (baseballs, bats, jerseys, etc.), most sellers use UPS to ship and insure their items.

But again, it is your choice, since you must feel secure in your decision. Also keep in mind that most buyers want their item to be shipped to them as cheaply as possible, within reason, but also want expensive items to be covered

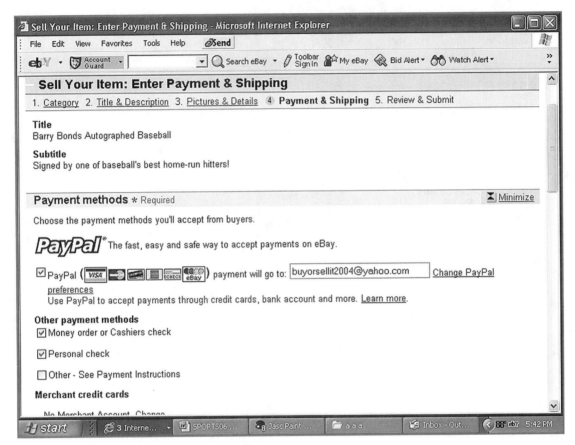

Figure 6.19

Accurate shipping information is important to buyers who might use this information to decide whether to bid in your auction, or in another seller's listing for the same item.

by insurance in case of damage or loss. You need to indicate every detail of shipping and its associated costs during the listing process.

At the bottom of this same screen, you can scroll down and see that eBay asks you to input information regarding payment instructions and return policy, as well as listing the locations you agree to ship to. Again, both of these sections depend on your own personal preference. While some sellers will ship anything anywhere in the world, others (such as yours truly) opt not to ship items outside of the United States due to time-consuming customs forms and the hassle of figuring out how much it costs to ship a framed 8×10 to France or Japan, and then having the winning buyer balk at paying for what figures to be a costly shipment. To me, it's just not worth it. It's up to you to decide.

A word of caution: You should provide accurate and reasonable shipping costs when you list your item for auction. If you are selling a signed baseball and designate your shipping cost at $25.00 (when it should cost you no more than $10–$12, including insurance), you're going to either not get many bids, get some angry emails from your winning bidder (if he did not notice the inflated amount before placing his bid), or worse yet, get negative feedback for the transaction. And negative feedback should be avoided at all costs if you plan to continue to sell on eBay!

If you have any questions about how much to charge for shipping, check out some listings by other sellers for similar items on eBay before making up your mind. The experienced, successful sellers know they must keep their shipping costs in line to keep their customers coming back for more.

Next, after carefully making all your shipping determinations, click on Continue. That should bring you up to the next screen (see Figure 6.20), which will give you your first look at how your item will be displayed on eBay.

The Home Stretch

You are getting close to getting your item ready for bids on eBay! All that remains is checking over your listing to see if it meets up with your expectations and if everything you input is accurate. You will have the option to change anything that doesn't seem just right by clicking in the proper area.

Step 1: A quick scroll through the page will show you the item title and description, the images you have linked to the auction, and the payment and shipping information (see Figure 6.21) that you have chosen for this item.

Step 2: If everything looks okay to this point, it is time to review the fees that you will be charged to list this item for auction (see Figure 6.22).

In this case, you would be paying a sum total of $2.65 in listing fees. The fees for listing an item for sale (insertion fees; see Figure 6.23) and for reserve price auctions (see Figure 6.24) vary according to a sliding scale based on list price.

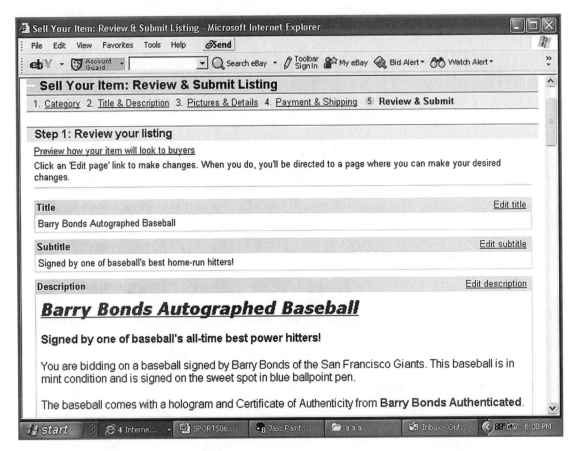

Figure 6.20

Review and submit: Check out the listing to see if it is accurate and meets with your approval.

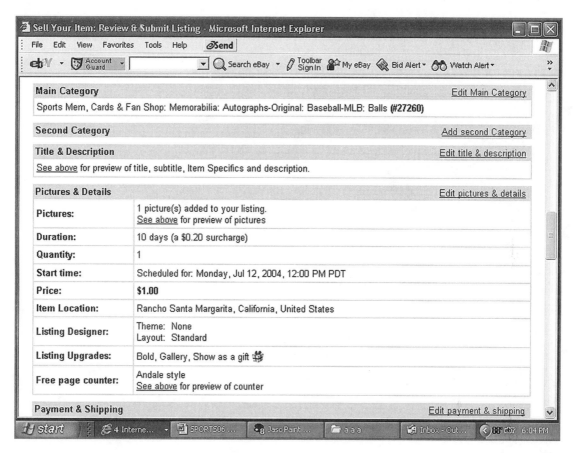

Figure 6.21

Double-check to make sure all the information is accurate in the listing.

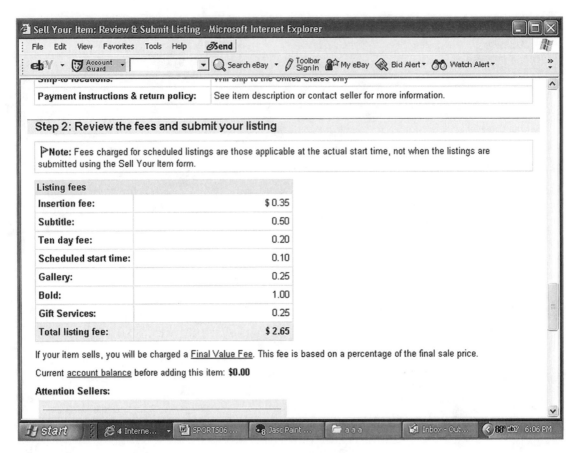

Figure 6.22

This section allows you to review the fees associated with listing your item.

Starting Price, Opening Value or Reserve Price	Insertion Fee
$0.01 - $0.99	$0.30
$1.00 - $9.99	$0.35
$10.00 - $24.99	$0.60
$25.00 - $49.99	$1.20
$50.00 - $199.99	$2.40
$200.00 - $499.99	$3.60
$500.00 and up	$4.80

Figure 6.23

This chart lists the graduated listing fees for inserting an auction on eBay according to opening value or reserve price.

Additional Reserve Price Auction fee (fully refunded if item sells):	
Reserve Price	**Reserve Price Auction Fee**
$0.01 - $49.99	$1.00
$50.00 - $199.99	$2.00
$200.00 and up	1% of Reserve Price (with a maximum of $100.00)

Figure 6.24

This chart lists the listing fees for reserve-price auctions; the fees are refunded if the item sells.

As the seller, you also will be charged a percentage of the final selling price; see Figure 6.25. You are not charged a final value fee if there are no bids on your item or there were no bids that met your reserve prices. But whether you finalize the sale with the buyer or not, you still are subject to a final value fee.

Closing Value	Final Value Fee
$0 - $25	5.25% of the closing value
$25 - $1,000	5.25% of the initial $25 ($1.31), plus 2.75% of the remaining closing value balance ($25.01 to $1,000)
Over $1,000	5.25% of the initial $25 ($1.31), plus 2.75% of the initial $25 - $1000 ($26.81), plus 1.50% of the remaining closing value balance ($1000.01 - closing value)

Figure 6.25

Use this chart to figure out what you will be charged as eBay's percentage of the final sale price.

Be advised that before you submit any autographed item to auction, eBay warns sellers about issues relating to authentication; see Figure 6.26. In a nutshell, eBay wants you to be aware that:

- Autographed items, commonly bought and sold on eBay, are unique in that they can be highly valuable yet easily forged. eBay strives to maintain a marketplace that is safe for both buyers and sellers of autographs, and has developed the following guidelines to protect you.

- Autographs are commonly sold with so-called Certificates of Authenticity (COA), which are designed to offer the buyer some assurances that the autograph was indeed properly signed by the person(s) in question. However, COAs are only as valuable as the reputation of the issuing party. Literally anyone can offer a COA, so it is important that savvy buyers investigate the background of each authenticator. Blank COAs are not permitted and certificates of authenticity may never be sold as a stand-alone item.

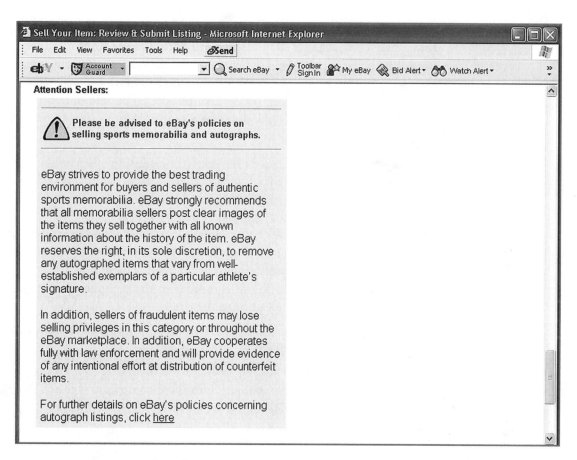

Figure 6.26

eBay makes it clear it will not tolerate auctions for autographs that are not properly authenticated. Be sure to follow the guidelines or your item might be removed from the auction listings.

- There are indeed reputable autograph experts and eBay has identified a partial list of such authenticators for your benefit. Such authenticators offer various services for buyers and sellers of autographs.

- eBay reserves the right, in its sole discretion, to remove any autographed item listed on its site and refund the associated listing fee, if eBay believes that the listing of the item is inconsistent with eBay's goal of providing a safe trading environment, or if in its sole discretion eBay believes that the sale of the item might create liability for the buyer, the seller, or any third party.

- An opinion from a disinterested third party regarding any autograph listing may be sought by eBay. If the third party has any concerns about the authenticity of the listing, eBay may at its sole discretion, remove the listing from the site. Sellers whose autographs have been repeatedly identified as problematic may be warned, put on probation, or suspended from all eBay buying and selling activity, at eBay's sole discretion.

- All autograph sellers are urged to include in their listings all relevant information known about the autograph and the item it appears on, including a clear scanned image of the actual autographed item for sale. If a seller promotes that an autograph comes with a "certificate of authenticity," the seller must include in the listing all relevant information about the certificate, including the name of the person or company issuing the certificate. eBay also highly recommends including a scan of the certificate. Listings that do not comply with these requirements may, at eBay's discretion, be removed from the site.

- A list of unacceptable authenticators who have run into trouble during federal investigations by the FBI and U.S. Attorneys' offices in San Diego and Chicago is provided by eBay. Any listings that refer to examinations or certificates of authenticity from these companies will not be allowed. For a list of banned sellers, see Chapter 4, "Authentication Is Sweeping the Nation."

At the bottom of the screen is the magic button. If you are ready to put your item on the auction block, click on the Submit button.

Ta da! Your item is now ready for bidding. See Figure 6.27.

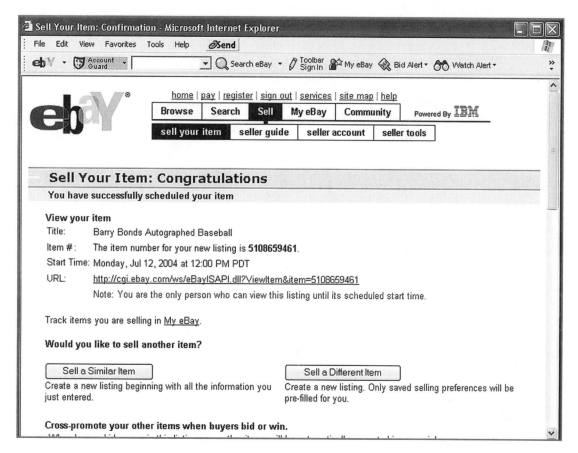

Figure 6.27

Congratulations! Your auction is ready for bidding!

chapter 7

The Auction Process

So far you've gone over the steps involved on how to list an item for sale. When your item is up for bid, it is being looked over by millions of eBay users all over the world. Kind of a neat feeling, no? If you agreed to international bidding, don't be surprised if you get emails about your item from someone in England, Australia, the Far East, and Mexico: Remember, collecting sports memorabilia is a popular pastime the world over. Sports fans all over the globe can watch the World Series, Super Bowl, Stanley Cup Playoffs, NBA Championship, World Cup, and pretty much any big sporting event just by tuning in the right channel on their television sets. They may sound a bit different depending on the dialect, but names like Jordan, Clemens, Marino, and Elway roll off the tongues of collectors speaking dozens of different languages.

Next I will guide you through the process of monitoring bids on your auctions, keeping the lines of communication open between you and interested bidders, learning to cross-merchandise your auctions, and doing your utmost to publicize your product.

Whether you plan to spend several hours a week selling on eBay or whether you plan to list just one item a week, these auction guidelines apply and can help make your eBay experience as painless and profitable as possible.

And another reminder: Don't forget to do your homework! If you read something in this book that sounds like it might come in handy again later on, get out your marking pen and highlight that section. It never hurts to go over the information again until it becomes embedded in the eBay game plan that lives in your heart and your head!

Can I Help You?

Selling sports memorabilia on eBay is pretty much the same as selling sports memorabilia in a store or at the mall. If you walked into a baseball card shop and the owner never looked up to answer questions you might have about an item in his store, or replied abruptly and just plain came off as unfriendly, you'd be apt to walk right out the door and look for another place to spend your money, wouldn't you?

The same selling principles apply to eBay. If you have an item for auction, it's just like having a baseball card shop. And when potential buyers click your listing, they are entering your shop to look around, most likely with cash (or credit card) in hand and hopefully with the intent of buying. Yes, there figures to be plenty of "lookey-loos" just doing some window-shopping, and some of the folks who email you won't be serious buyers. But that's the sales world. Still, you never know who's going to be buying what and how much of it until after the merchandise and money have officially traded hands. Remember to keep a smile on your face (or at least make your email replies sound friendly and respectful) and treat everybody the same.

A perfect non-eBay example: At one sports card show recently, I had set up a fairly large display booth with all sorts of pro basketball merchandise, ranging from inexpensive autographed 8×10 photos to more costly game-used and signed equipment that almost all show shoppers love to stop, look at, and admire, but few actually want or have enough money on hand to purchase. Particularly of interest at this show were a pair of LeBron James game-used and signed basketball shoes, in addition to a game-used Los Angeles Lakers jersey once worn by star player and TV/movie actor Rick Fox. Hundreds, and perhaps thousands, of interested and astonished buyers came by to ogle these rare items, often calling over their friends or family members to take a look. For 99.9 percent of them, this might be the closest they ever came to touching and feeling memorabilia once actually used by the heroes they worship on the basketball court.

One day, a young father in his early 20s happened to come by the booth, pushing a stroller that contained his hotdog-eating toddler, who couldn't have been more than 4 years of age. Remembering those days myself, when it was more important to spend precious funds on diapers than on sports cards and memorabilia, I offered the father and his son a free LeBron James basketball trading card as a friendly gesture. To my surprise, the father quickly looked away from me and continued slowing walking along the booth, preferring instead to just continue looking at the merchandise.

No problem, I thought, since not everyone collects basketball cards, and maybe this young parent preferred not to accept my handout. But what happened next shocked me.

Once this young father got to the end of the booth, he slowly swung the stroller around and headed back to the center of the display, where I was standing. "How much for the LeBron shoes and the Fox jersey?" he asked. "What's the best deal you can give me if I take both right now?" Needless to say, the questions from what now seemed to be the collector-dad surprised me, so after a few seconds of contemplation, I offered to discount the deal $2,000 if he would buy both items.

Without even batting an eye, the young father reached in his pocket for his wallet and pulled out his American Express card. A few minutes later we had completed the sale for the pair of items for $2,000. He was happy, I was happy, and a sale that I never suspected would take place had been completed in a matter of minutes.

The point is this: When you're a salesman, you really never know what's going to happen. If you treat people with respect and answer their questions honestly and in a timely manner, the same type of sales outcome as described earlier can happen to you one day. It's a good idea to keep tabs on your auction items and answer all email questions you receive from prospective buyers.

Questions and Answers

Revisit the example item you listed previously on eBay (see Chapter 6, "Getting Ready to Sell"). The baseball autographed by Barry Bonds is up for sale, and when somebody clicks your auction listing, they will see all the information you input previously (see Figure 7.1).

If a bidder has a question, he will maneuver over to the Seller Information box (see Figure 7.2), where he will find a link that says Ask Seller a Question. By clicking that link, eBay directs him to another screen that will allow him to ask whatever questions he has about the item (see Figure 7.3).

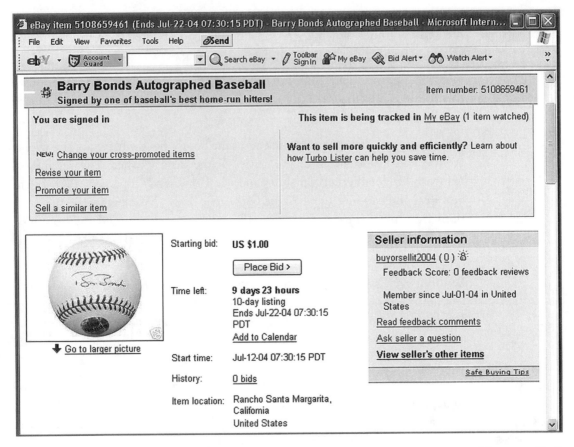

Figure 7.1

All the information input during the listing process can be viewed on the auction page.

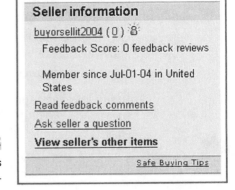

Figure 7.2

This is where buyers will find the link to ask questions about your auction.

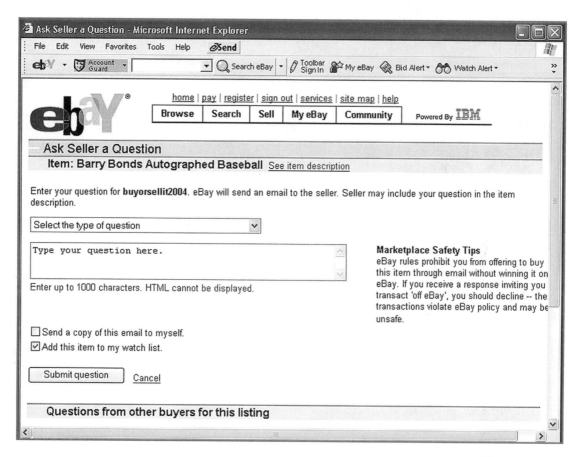

Figure 7.3

The buyer can fill out his question about your item by using this form.

A prospective buyer can ask the seller a general question about the item or a question about shipping policy. He can also check the box that allows him to receive a copy of the email question, too (see Figure 7.4). He can also add the item you are selling to his watch list.

Once the question field has been filled out and the bidder clicks the Submit Question button, the eBay machinery goes into motion. It triggers an email to be sent to the address you have on account for this user ID. You will receive an email from your interested buyer (see Figure 7.5), which allows you to simply reply with the answer. Be sure to read the email carefully and answer as honestly and as promptly as possible. It's a good idea to be square with the

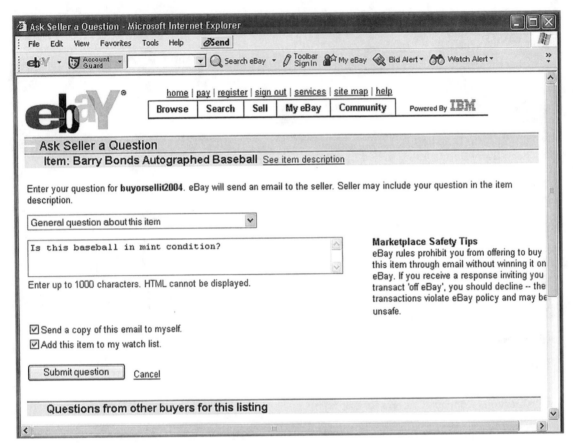

Figure 7.4

A buyer has the option of adding your item to his watch list.

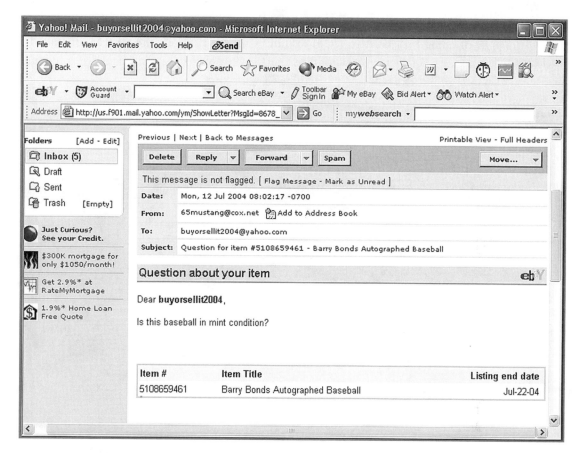

Figure 7.5

The buyer's question will be sent to the seller in an email.

potential bidder even if you don't know the answer to his question; either that or email him back to let him know you will find out the answer for him. It's almost 100 percent guaranteed that if you do not answer emails from bidders, those bidders will not participate in your auction.

You can monitor the bids in your auction by simply clicking the listing on eBay (see Figure 7.6).

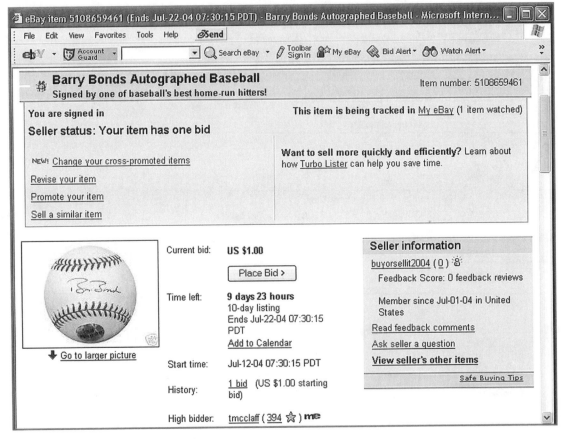

Figure 7.6

It's a good idea to monitor the bids on your auctions.

Oops . . . Can I Change That?

What happens if you made a mistake on your listing? You are able to revise anything pertaining to your auction as long as nobody has bid on it yet. You would simply click the Revise Your Item button at the top of the listing (again, see Figure 7.6). You are allowed to revise anything in your listing except the selling format (e.g., you can't switch your item from being in an auction to a store) if your item has received no bids and the auction listing does not end within the next 12 hours.

But what if there are bids on the item, and more than 12 hours left in the auction? That changes things a bit. Now eBay only allows you to add to your item's description. If you have made a mistake or need to add some vital information to the listing, follow these steps:

1. Click the Revise Your Item button at the top of the page.

    That will bring up a new form, in which to provide your updates (see Figure 7.7). Here, you will see that the next eBay screen automatically enters the number of the auction you last had up on your screen.

2. Clicking Continue brings up another display in which you can add the information you want.

    In this case, the Barry Bonds autographed baseball you had earlier listed for sale has already had a bid on it. If your item does have bids, you can only add to the item description or add optional features (such as bold-facing your listing) for additional fees to help increase your auction's visibility among buyers.

3. If you click Continue, it will bring up another new screen (see Figure 7.8) that informs you that you are revising your item.

4. Scroll down to the bottom of the page and locate the area that says Add to Description (see Figure 7.9).

5. Click the Add to Description link and you will be prompted with a new screen (see Figure 7.10) in which to type in whatever the message is that you'd like your bidders to know.

When you revise an auction that has bids on it, the eBay system will post a time/date stamp with your revision so a buyer knows exactly when that information has been added to the listing (see Figure 7.11). This is particularly

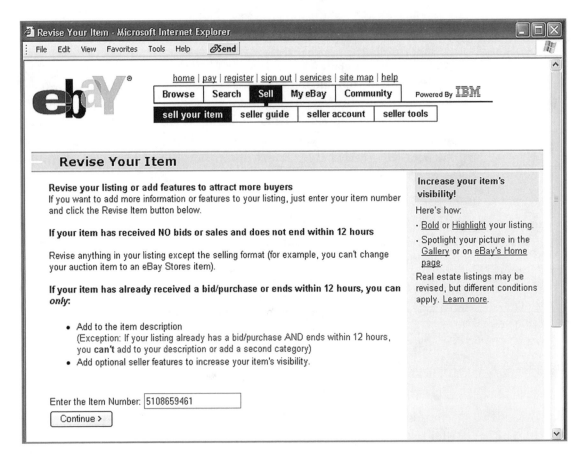

Figure 7.7

You can revise or update your item and even add optional selling features to increase your auction's visibility among bidders.

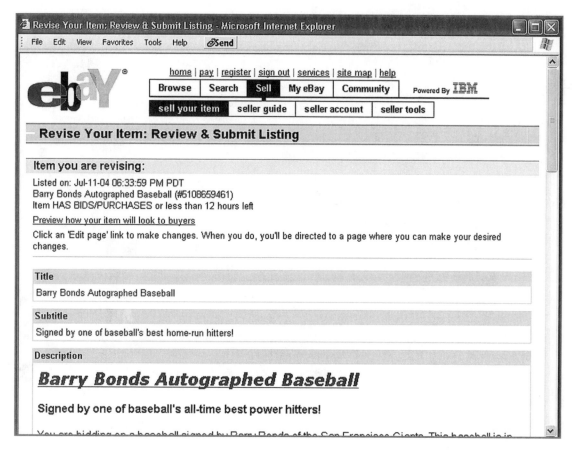

Figure 7.8

Here is where you will begin to revise any information that needs correcting.

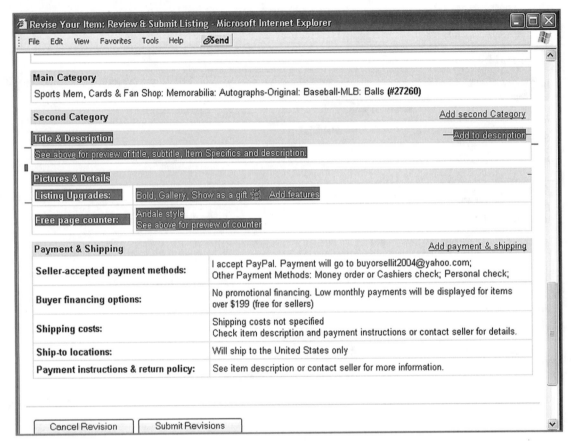

Figure 7.9

Type in the information you think buyers might need to know in order to convince them to bid in your auction.

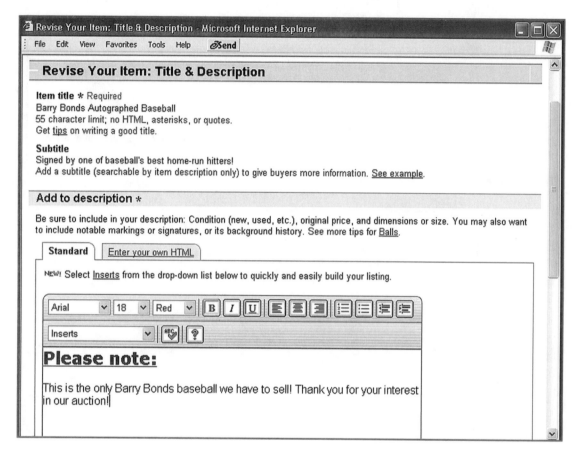

Figure 7.10

You can use the eBay font, point size, and color options to liven up your listing here, too.

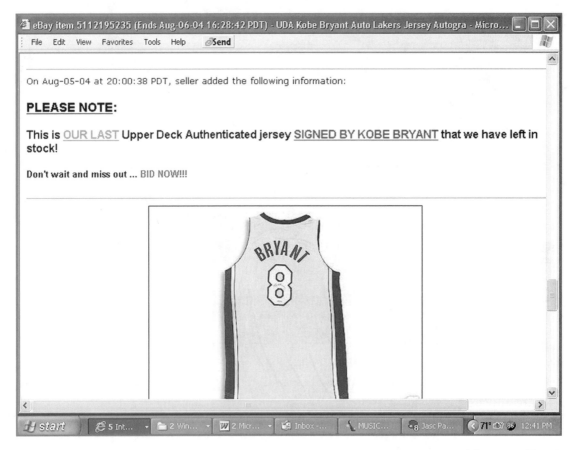

On Aug-05-04 at 20:00:38 PDT, seller added the following information:

PLEASE NOTE:

This is OUR LAST Upper Deck Authenticated jersey SIGNED BY KOBE BRYANT that we have left in stock!

Don't wait and miss out ... BID NOW!!!

Figure 7.11

The date and time of your revision or addition is noted in the listing if you make the changes after bids have already been made. Here's a time-stamped update for a Kobe Bryant jersey.

helpful should the information you add come into question later on. If the winning bidder placed his bid after you added the information, the sale then would be subject to any updates to the terms or description. Basically, the winning buyer couldn't say he didn't know something, if it's right there with a date and time on it.

Maybe This Would Interest You, Too

If you plan to sell a lot on eBay, one of the best ways to get even more bids on your auctions is to cross-merchandise. eBay simplifies this process by actually listing other items you have for sale (see Figure 7.12) within the second half of an auction page. If a buyer clicks your auction listing, he will see some of the other items you have for sale, too.

You also can click the Seller: Change Your Cross-Promoted Items link within that feature to match up items that you think might also interest a buyer. For instance, if you have an auction for a Boston Celtics team-signed basketball and

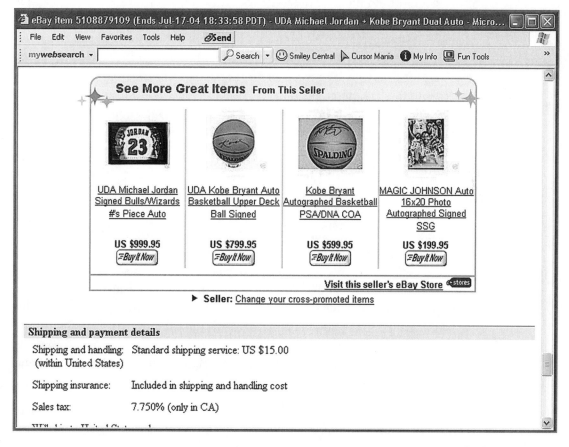

Figure 7.12

Cross-merchandising is an effective way of letting buyers know what else you have for sale.

you have another auction for a Larry Bird rookie basketball card, you might want to cross-merchandise these two listings with each other. Odds are, a buyer interested enough to click the Celtics team ball probably would like to take a look at the Bird rookie card, too. It's worth spending the time it takes to link products that might work together and let your customers know about other items you have for sale—just like in the grocery store. (It's not an accident the potato chips and canned soda are in the same aisle now, is it?) It's just good business. And there is no additional charge for cross-promoting your items.

Who's Doing the Bidding?

It's a good idea to monitor the feedback on the buyers who are bidding in your auctions. Even though 99 times out of a 100 you probably won't have any problems, every once in a while a knucklehead comes out of nowhere and can cause you some heavy-duty headaches. If you see a buyer with little or no feedback starting to place bids on several of your auctions, click his feedback rating. If he is new to eBay, he might not yet have had much of a chance to run up a good rating yet. But if he has been bidding for a long time (by clicking the feedback rating in parentheses, the buyer's location and original eBay registration date is displayed, as you can see in Figure 7.13), has more than a couple negative feedback comments, or has retracted one or more bids in recent weeks, it might be wise to email or call the bidder to see just how serious he is about actually buying your item.

Sometimes, bidding in auctions brings out the kid in some people. Or just brings out the kids, period. And the last thing you want to have happen is to be holding up a big sale, waiting for a payment that will never arrive. That also could mean a serious bidder who was the runner-up in the auction has quickly moved on to other items or other sellers, and that can cost you a big sale with a legitimate customer. But before you start canceling bids by new users, it's good etiquette to check with them first. (You can find in-depth information about canceling bids at http://offer.ebay.com/ws/eBayISAPI.dll?CancelBid-Show.)

Weeding out nonpayers, game players, and bid retractors will make eBay a nicer place to do business for both you and your bidders.

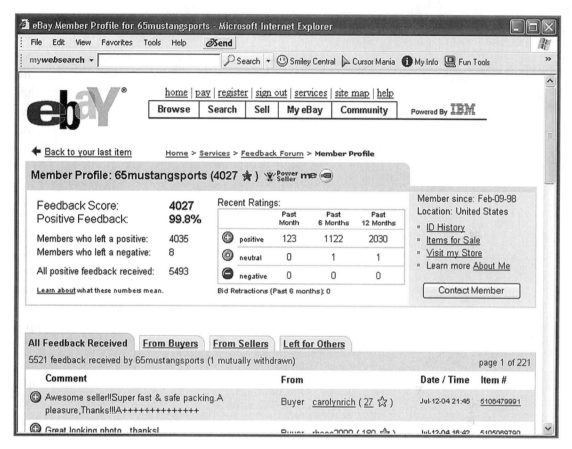

Figure 7.13

A bidder's history is available on the same page where you'd find his feedback rating.

Come Visit My Store

Another way of promoting your business is visible when you click the feedback rating; see Figure 7.13. If you click the link that says Visit My Store, a buyer is directed to your eBay storefront. An eBay store, shown in Figure 7.14, is a terrific way to maximize your business potential on eBay. You get several benefits:

■ Access to tools that help you create your own brand name on eBay.

■ A brand name, which gives most buyers more confidence in you as a seller.

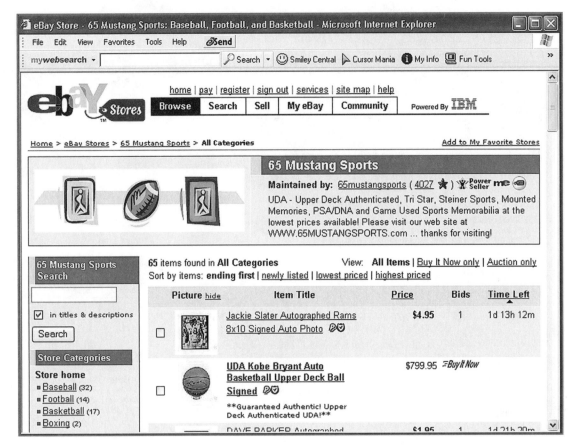

Figure 7.14

If you have a lot of merchandise to sell, then opening up an eBay Store is probably a good idea. It's a wonderful way for buyers to shop through your other items.

- Store listings also are designed to last longer (30, 60, 90, or 120 days, or "Good 'Til Cancelled").

- Cheaper listings (usually just a few cents per listing) than regular eBay listings.

They work very similar to the Buy It Now listings. You name your price for the item in your store, and if somebody goes shopping there and sees something he wants to buy at the price you have set, you have a match.

All of this can mean bigger profits, too. Plus, you have access to some professional-looking storefront tools that make shopping easier for your buyers. If you have your own web site, you can link buyers to it through your eBay store—and master using the cross-promotion tool, too.

All store sellers receive monthly sales reports that outline their activity by category (monthly gross sales, conversion rates, or number of buyers, for example). Additionally, if you have a featured or anchor store, you'll also receive overall eBay marketplace data to benchmark your sales with other eBay sellers.

Besides, you can try an eBay store and the first 30 days are free. How can you top that?

chapter 8

Closing the Deal

Like a champion three-year-old thoroughbred at the Kentucky Derby, your auction now is headed down the final stretch. An item that you listed for sale only a few days ago—an Eric Gagne L.A. Dodgers bobble head doll—now has just a few minutes left on the clock. The finish line is finally in sight. And just like Gagne, you are ready to close out a victory.

You click the auction listing and the seconds are ticking down . . . 30, 29, 28, 27 . . . you refresh your screen and now there are fewer than 10 seconds to go . . . 5, 4, 3, 2, 1 . . . the auction has ended!

Congratulations, you have made your first sale on eBay.

There still is more work to be done. The next steps will be to confirm the payment process to your buyer, pack and ship the item in a safe manner, leave appropriate feedback for your buyer, and keep the lines of communication open. The next section also will help you deal with nonpaying bidders and provide some tips about relisting your item for sale if the circumstances so dictate. These steps might at first seem tedious, but they are all keys to becoming a successful seller on eBay.

Congratulations! You've Made a Sale!

The auction is now over and some lucky bidder is the new owner of your merchandise, but your work has just begun. If you refresh the page showing your listing one more time (see Figure 8.1), all the final details of the sale will come into view. In the example shown in the figure, the bidding has ended at $15.95.

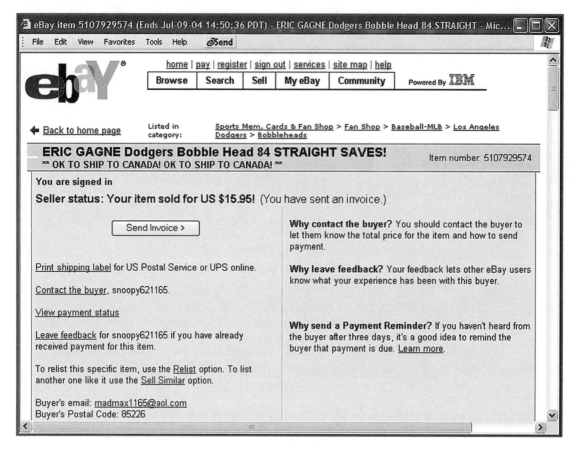

Figure 8.1

Once an auction is completed, pertinent information is available to the seller and winning bidder.

At this point, it is time to send an invoice to your winning bidder so that you can get paid and get his item shipped out as soon as possible.

The Send Invoice button appears just below the line that says Seller Status. Click that button. What pops up next on your screen (see Figure 8.2) is a formed called Send Invoice to Buyer. The form includes the name of your auction, auction number, the winning bid amount, and the shipping fee that you originally listed when you put the item up for sale.

If you scroll down to the bottom of the page, you can click the button that says Send Invoice. This will automatically trigger an email that's sent to your win-

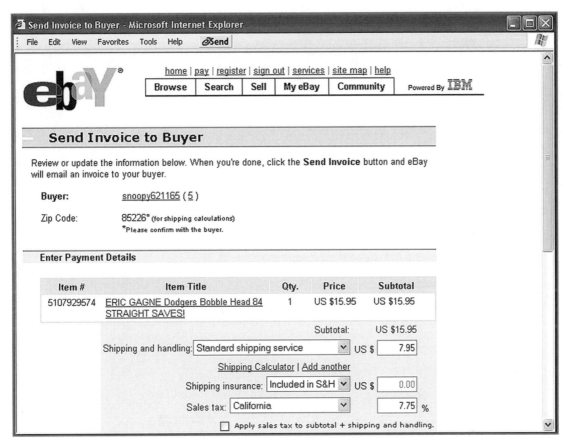

Figure 8.2

The eBay invoice will include shipping and sales tax, if applicable.

ning bidder. That email will contain the details of the eBay invoice. You also will see on the next screen that pops up (see Figure 8.3), in which eBay confirms to you that an invoice has been sent to the buyer. If you have clicked the box at the bottom of the invoice page (again, see Figure 8.2) to copy you on the invoice, then you too should have received an email with the invoice information. That information is shown in Figure 8.4. The buyer is informed of the payment address if he is going to mail a check or money order, and he also can click a link within the email to pay you via PayPal if you have listed that as an option for your item.

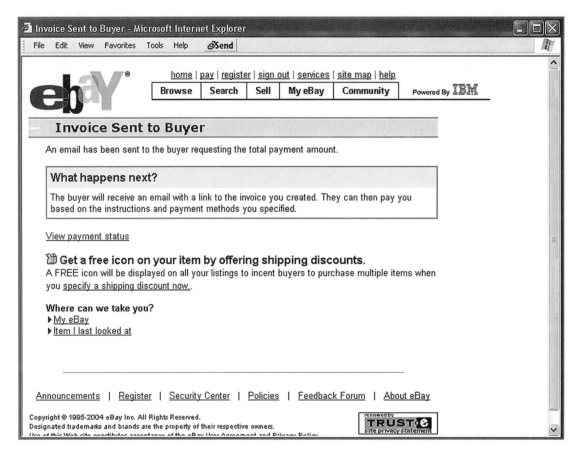

Figure 8.3

This is the confirmation screen that informs a seller that an invoice has been successfully sent to a buyer.

The Payment Process

By now, the buyer has received email confirmation from eBay that he has won your auction. If you have sent the eBay invoice, then he has received payment information from you. It's up to you to get in touch with your buyer to complete the sale. You need to let the buyer know what the shipping cost is, any sales tax for the purchase, if applicable, and how you will ship the item. You will have to make sure to ask the buyer for the address to which he'd like the item shipped.

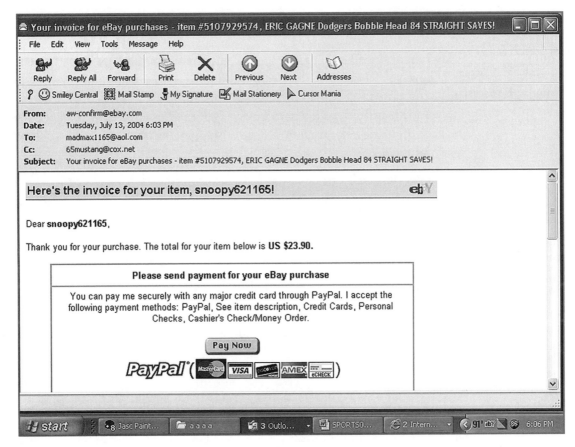

Figure 8.4

Both the seller and buyer can receive email invoices through eBay.

Buyers are more likely to bid on your items if your auction listing clearly states all alternative payment methods, such as checks or money orders. If there are specific types of payment you don't accept, say so. You can also employ the eBay shipping calculator in your listing if you so choose, and you should spell out your return policy on the item. Letting buyers know they can return or exchange the item for a working replacement boosts sales and final selling prices.

Tips on Shipping

Every step of the eBay selling process is important, but perhaps none more so than how you choose to ship your product. If your item receives damage because of how you shipped it, you probably will have lost a future customer. The recipient will be less likely to buy again from you, even if the damage was the fault of the carrier, not you. The right shipping solutions can help you save time and money.

As you decide which carrier to use, take into consideration the type of services offered. While you may primarily use ground transportation, it's a good idea to consider offering these options:

■ Next-day or second-day air service when the customer needs to receive the item right away (as a last-second gift, for example).

■ Three-day delivery for time-sensitive packages on a cost-sensitive budget.

■ Some carriers even offer guaranteed day-definite ground delivery (so that both you and the recipient know exactly when the package will arrive).

One of the nicer innovations eBay has come up with is the links to United Parcel Service (UPS) and the United States Postal Service (USPS) right from the listing page of your auction. You can pay for these shipping services online and have the funds deducted directly from your PayPal account. No need to write a check at the end of the month or stand in line at the post office. Now that's a beautiful thing!

You also have the option of signing up for accounts with the post office (www.usps.com) and with UPS (www.ups.com) if you so choose. Either way, you will be able to provide online tracking information (usually by email) to help notify your customer that his package is on its way. You can also request that your package be signed for by your customer to ensure proper delivery, but be prepared to pay for every extra service you plan to use. Shipping supplies also can be ordered online through these two web sites.

Usually, the best way to ship a single sports card (since it only weighs a few ounces) is by the post office. Be certain to insure it if it has a significant value (usually over $50). It should also be enclosed in a protective plastic top-loader (or protective plastic capsule if it has been graded) along with bubble wrap. Using a shipping envelope already lined with bubble wrap is recommended, too.

When it comes to shipping sports memorabilia, many times it is easier and less expensive to ship by UPS, which offers ground service and expedited air shipping if so desired by you and your customer. Also, you can purchase insurance for your package online through UPS, while insurance for items shipped by USPS must be purchased at the post office window. If you have several packages, and if the line at your local post office is as long as it usually is at mine, this is another good reason to go with UPS on insured packages.

International shipping costs vary greatly depending on what, where, and how you are shipping. Generally, buyers pay additional costs that may apply such as duties, taxes, and customs clearance fees. For example, international rates may or may not include pickup and door-to-door delivery with customs clearance. If you decide to ship by USPS, you can offer your buyer delivery by Global Priority Mail, Global Express Mail, Airmail, and regular parcel post (which is the least expensive, but slowest way to ship).

If you are shipping larger packages that weigh 150 pounds or more, you probably should consider using the eBay freight resource center, where you can find helpful tips and sign up for a free account at www.freightquote.com to receive discount rates and personalized service.

When shipping a larger package, you should remember to follow the steps below to help prevent damage during transit:

■ Always wrap items with plenty of cushioning. You can use bubble wrap, foam peanuts, corrugated dividers, crumpled packing paper, or crumpled newspaper. Foam peanuts sometimes will shift during transit, so be sure to pack your box as full as possible if using this material.

■ Use a sturdy box with rigid sides and plenty of room for cushioning on all sides. Every box is designed and constructed to hold a maximum gross weight, and that weight usually is printed on the box.

■ Be sure to securely seal your package with shipping or packing tape. Masking, cellophane, or duct tape is not recommended.

■ Put yourself in your buyer's place. How would you want your package to arrive at your doorstep if you were the winning bidder? If your item were damaged because your seller had cut corners, wouldn't you be a bit upset? Keep this in mind as you prepare your item to be packed inside the back of a big tractor-trailer rig or air container.

■ Check with your shipping service for specific requirements and packaging limitations. If you need to file an insurance claim later on, you need to know what their requirements are. Otherwise, you might be in for a big disappointment (and a substantial monetary loss).

Leaving Feedback for Buyers

If you are hoping to build up a good feedback record on eBay, a good way to start is to be certain to leave feedback for others involved in transactions with you. The feedback forum shown in Figure 8.5 is designed to help you rate your trading partners and help inform others what your experience was like.

Every eBay member has a profile in the feedback forum. A profile has basic information about the member and a list of feedback left by their trading partners from previous transactions. Learning to trust a member of the community has a lot to do with what his or her customers or sellers have to say!

For each transaction, only the buyer and seller can rate each other by leaving feedback. Each feedback left consists of a positive, negative, or neutral rating and a short comment. Leaving honest comments about a particular eBay member gives other community members a good idea of what to expect when dealing with that member. Once it is left, the feedback becomes a permanent part of the member's profile.

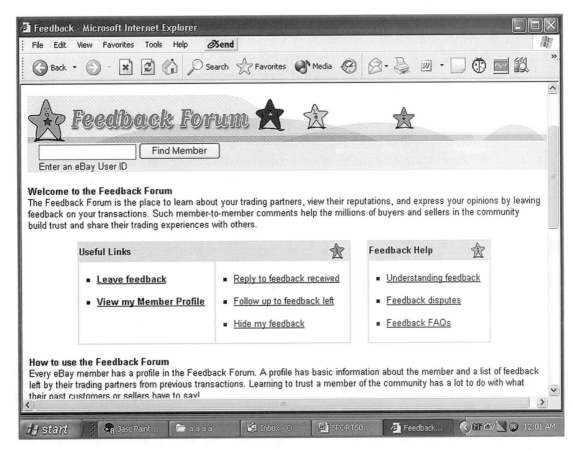

Figure 8.5

The feedback forum can help you keep track of past experiences with buyers. It can help you build trust with your customers.

Alert

Sometimes feedback becomes a cat-and-mouse game. Some sellers won't leave feedback for you until you leave feedback for them, fearing unwanted negative comments. It also sometimes works the other way, with buyers not leaving feedback for a transaction, successful or not, until the seller provides a nice comment first. It's up to you to decide what to do, but I have found that leaving positive feedback in a timely manner encourages buyers to shop through your auctions again, sooner rather than later. It's simply good auction etiquette.

Feedback ratings are used to determine each member's feedback score. A positive rating adds 1 to the score, a negative rating decreases it by 1, and a neutral rating has no impact. The higher the feedback score, the more positive ratings they've received from members. However, a member can increase or decrease another member's score by only 1 no matter how many transactions they share.

The feedback score and the corresponding feedback star are shown next to the every member's user ID. A feedback score of at least 10 earns you a yellow star (see Figure 8.6). As your feedback score increases, you can earn different colored stars—all the way to a red shooting star for a score above 100,000. Your star is your symbol of trust and experience in the eBay community.

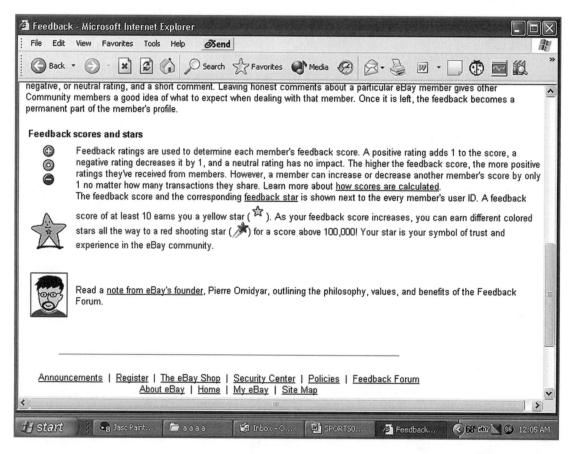

Figure 8.6

An eBay user receives different colored stars according to his feedback rating.

Second-Chance Offers

Sellers can send second-chance offers to any of the losing bidders in three cases:

- The winning bidder does not pay the seller.
- A seller has duplicate items.
- The reserve price is not met in a reserve price auction.

Second-chance offers can be created immediately after a listing ends for up to 60 days afterward.

Be advised that eBay recommends that sellers ensure that everything has been done to resolve the issue with a nonpaying bidder before sending a second-chance offer to another bidder.

Best of all, creating a second-chance offer is free! Sellers pay only the final value fee if the buyer accepts the second-chance offer. And, for reserve price auctions that do not meet the reserve price, the reserve price insertion fee will be automatically credited when the offer is accepted.

A second-chance offer can be sent to buyers in a one-, three-, five-, or seven-day duration. The one-day duration option has been added to offer sellers increased flexibility and convenience when using a second-chance offer.

Dealing with Nonpayment

The key to successful sales on eBay is direct communication between sellers and buyers. However, from time to time, misunderstandings occur.

If you have a nonpaying buyer and want to get a final value fee credit, follow these four steps:

1. Contact your buyer.
2. Send a payment reminder.
3. File a nonpaying bidder alert. This is the same for auction-style listings and Buy It Now.
4. Request a Final Value Fee credit.

As of July, 2004, eBay has instituted a new Non-Paying Buyer process. The new system was designed to enable sellers and buyers to successfully complete a transaction and reduce the amount of work required to file for Final Value Fee credit. Instead of a mandatory waiting period, a seller can receive a Final Value Fee credit much quicker under the new criteria. You also receive that credit immediately if the buyer is no longer a registered eBay user at the time the seller files the claim, or if the buyer is from a country to which the seller has designated he will not ship to.

The seller can first file an Unpaid Item Reminder seven days after the listing closes. This reminder starts a set of onsite and email communications from eBay to the buyer reminding them that it is time to pay, giving instructions on how to do so, and allowing for communication with the seller.

Second, the seller can file a Mutual Agreement Not to Proceed. This option prompts the buyer to confirm the agreement. Once the buyer does so, eBay issues a Final Value Fee credit to the seller. The seller also receives a Final Value Fee credit if the buyer fails to respond in seven days (and the buyer receives a strike). The seller can end communication at any time and receive their credit.

Thus, a bidder who receives a nonpaying bidder alert does not get off free if he does not pay for the auction. eBay states that buyers automatically enter into a legally binding contract to purchase the item once they bid, and they must pay for the items they commit to purchase. If a buyer gets too many "strikes" in too short a time period (not spelled out in detail by eBay), his account can be suspended indefinitely, though he also has the right to appeal should suspension occur. Sellers are always encouraged by eBay to issue nonpaying bidder alerts for buyers who try to skirt the system, because this is about the only way for system abusers to get booted off the web site.

Alert

Sellers who file false reports of unpaid items may be subject to suspension from eBay, so only file when you have an actual claim.

Remember that most nonpaying buyer situations are resolved through communication with the buyer. You can also try mediation, or just call the buyer. However, if the situation is not resolved with a completed sale and you relist the item, you may qualify for a refund on the relisted item's insertion fee.

What if My Item Doesn't Sell?

If your listing ended without a winning buyer or resulted in a nonpaying buyer the first time, you may qualify for a credit by relisting the item. If the item sells the second time, eBay will refund the insertion fee for the relisting.

To relist an item, follow along with these steps:

1. Sign in to eBay.

2. Go to the item page for the ended listing.

3. Click Relist Your Item.

There are a few general requirements for you to receive the credit:

- You must relist the item within 90 days of the original listing's closing date.

- Only the first relisting of an item is eligible. Subsequent relistings of the same item do not qualify.

- Both the original listing and the relisting must be in online auction or fixed-price format.

- Both the original listing and the relisting must be single quantity (not Dutch).

- The starting price you set for the relisted item must not be greater than that of the original listing.

- The relisted item can't have a reserve price if the original listing didn't have one. If it did, the reserve price you set for the relisted item must not be greater than that of the original listing.

- The relisted item must end with a winning buyer. If the item doesn't sell the second time, the insertion fee is not refunded.

If your original listing resulted in a nonpaying buyer:

■ Make sure you filed a nonpaying buyer alert for the original listing and requested a full Final Value Fee credit for that listing. This credit must be posted to your account before you can receive the insertion fee credit.

This offer only applies to the insertion fee, not to other fees for options such as bold, highlight, and so on. After your relisted item is sold, you will be charged the applicable fees.

Keeping in Touch

Even after you have sent your winning bidder an eBay invoice, received payment, shipped the item, and left feedback, it's not a bad idea to send the winning bidder a follow-up email later on. You can find the winning bidder's email address on the auction listing and send a short thank-you note that reinforces the fact that his item is in transit and that you have left positive feedback on the transaction. That way, the buyer is more apt to leave positive feedback for you once his package arrives, assuming he is satisfied with his item and how it was shipped. A little friendly touch sometimes can go a long way toward earning a customer's repeat business.

chapter 9

Next Steps

The key to success on buying or selling on eBay is to try, try again. If you are just starting out, you might not win that first auction—or the next three or four or dozen you decide to bid in. The same thing goes for selling. You may try to sell an item and get no bids at all, or see your auction end at a price way below what you were hoping for.

Don't get discouraged. The first time Tiger Woods swung a golf club, he didn't hit a hole-in-one. The first time Babe Ruth hit a baseball, it didn't go over the Grand Canyon. The first time Wayne Gretzky laced on his hockey skates, he fell face-down on the ice many, many times. The lesson here is to never give up: If the wonder and excitement and unpredictability of online auctions are what brought you to eBay in the first place, you shouldn't let a little disappointment get in the way. Just keep plugging along. It'll get better for you if you keep working at it.

Now, if you're already a seasoned pro (or at least have a fairly significant track record established on eBay) and are hoping to blossom even further, I still have some tips and tricks that can help you out. If your business grows to the point where you are a high-volume seller, eBay offers some tools that will help you manage your auction inventory.

When you feel ready to move up, you might consider giving Turbo Lister or Selling Manager a try. And even if you decide to continue "doing your own thing"—many sellers, myself included, have tried these many eBay tools but still prefer their own self-made systems—you could be in line to earn the title of eBay PowerSeller before long. PowerSellers enjoy several advantages over the rest of the eBay community, so if selling is your thing, that elite status is definitely something to shoot for.

Moving Up

For sellers who use eBay extensively, it won't hurt to check out some of the advanced selling tools that might help your business grow.

One of the new and improved bulk-listing tools offered by eBay is called Turbo Lister. This tool will help you create auction listings on your home computer. There is no charge to download or to use Turbo Lister (see Figure 9.1), and it

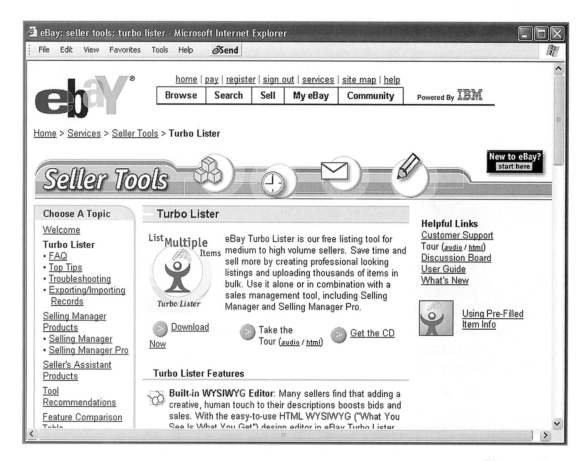

Figure 9.1

Turbo Lister is free to use and can help simplify typical workflow.

offers some helpful features that can streamline your labor, including a WYSIWYG (what you see is what you get) description editor, HTML templates, and the ability to schedule start times for listings. Turbo Lister was designed with the medium- to high-volume seller in mind. It can help you save time (which means you make more money!) by helping you design professional-looking auction listings and by simultaneously uploading as many auction items as you choose. You can also combine Turbo Lister—which can be used offline if you choose—with other sales-management tools, such as Selling Manager and Selling Manager Pro (both also offered by eBay).

With the WYSIWYG editor, you can lend your own touch to your descriptions, and that can help increase the amount bidders are willing to pay for your item. That also means more bidders may be apt to take a chance on your auction. More bids and higher bids mean better business for you.

The HTML templates offered in Turbo Lister also can come in handy. You can choose from a variety of predesigned layouts without even having to know anything about HTML (HyperText Markup Language). Personally, I sometimes enjoy the challenge of learning new things, so I discovered how to do HTML by the old try-and-fail method. It has been my choice not to use Turbo Lister, and I have survived six-plus years as a PowerSeller on eBay. But not everybody has the time or patience to figure out HTML, and so Turbo Lister definitely can speed things up for them, while minimizing the frustration level.

While using Turbo Lister is free, you should note that you still will be charged for your eBay listings, just as if you didn't use it at all. The seller is still responsible for paying fees related to listing insertion, final value, scheduled listings, and listing upgrades such as bold text or Gallery placement.

Selling Manager

eBay offers both Selling Manager and Selling Manager Pro for those who are looking for additional online selling tools. These options can help you perform all of your listing and sales-related activities from one location in My eBay. They were developed to meet the specific needs of medium- and high-volume sellers, with the goal of helping you manage your auctions as easily and efficiently as possible. eBay Selling Manager is a sales-management tool, not a listing device (see Figure 9.2).

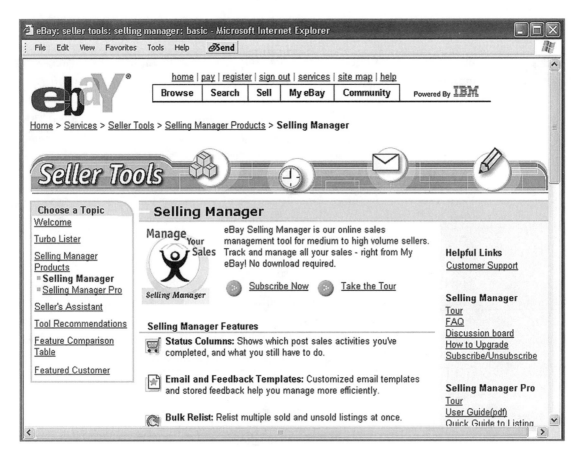

Figure 9.2

eBay Selling Manager can help expand your business and simplify many listing chores.

Selling Manager can help you do a plethora of things:

- Manage pending auctions that you want to have listed on eBay at a future date.

- Monitor your unsold inventory.

- Keep tabs on all of your active eBay listings.

- Manage feedback and email.

- Request payments from winning bidders.

- Download your sales history.

- Print shipping labels and invoices directly from sales records.

- Perform bulk chores relating to relisted items, feedback, and billing.

eBay Selling Manager is available via a monthly subscription. As a new user, you will have a one-month free trial. Your subscription fee will be $4.99 per month. That fee is automatically added to your eBay account and appears on your monthly invoice. You still are responsible for paying fees related to listing insertion, final value, scheduled listings, and listing upgrades such as bold text or Gallery placement.

PowerSellers: eBay's Stars

If you plan to sell a lot on eBay, one of your goals should be to earn PowerSeller status. PowerSellers are those who maintain a consistently high volume of monthly sales and a high level of total feedback (98 percent positive or better). They are recognized for their contributions to the success of eBay with a star system. When buyers see the PowerSeller icon next to a user ID, they know they are dealing with a seller who ranks among the most successful on eBay. PowerSellers consistently sell the most product and have attained the highest level of customer service.

There are five levels of PowerSellers: Bronze, Silver, Gold, Platinum, and Titanium (see Figure 9.3), each associated with different levels of monthly sales. Each level offers sellers a chance to enjoy benefits reserved just for them, including prioritized customer support (to help solve eBay-related problems), promotional offers, eBay promotional merchandise, special invitations to seller workshops and forums, opportunities to participate in research, and other special rewards (see Figure 9.4). Membership is free, as long as your track record as a seller meets the requirements.

To become a PowerSeller, you must have an active account on the eBay site for a minimum of 90 days. Then, you must average at least 4 listings over a 3-month period, all the time maintaining a minimum total feedback of 100 or more, including a 98 percent (or better) positive rating. You must also be sure to keep your eBay account current (with no outstanding balances) and comply with all eBay listing policies, while continuing to uphold the values (honesty, timeliness, and mutual respect) that earned you PowerSeller status in the first

Bronze	Silver	Gold	Platinum	Titanium
$1,000	$3,000	$10,000	$25,000	$150,000

Figure 9.3

PowerSellers can attain Bronze to Titanium status depending on their average monthly gross sales.

Tier	Priority eSupport	Toll Free Phone	Account Manager
Bronze	Yes		
Silver	Yes	Yes	
Gold	Yes	Yes	Yes
Platinum	Yes	Yes	Yes
Titanium	Yes	Yes	Yes

Figure 9.4

Each PowerSeller status offers different levels of support for the seller.

place. A minimum of $1,000 in gross monthly sales over a 3-month span also is required.

If you meet this criterion as a seller, expect to be invited to join the PowerSeller Club by emails sent out each month by eBay. There are advantages to joining the club. Through the PowerSeller program, eBay provides technical assistance for your eBay accounts and use of eBay online services.

Other advantages to joining the PowerSellers team include:

■ **Exclusive Offers**

■ eBay co-op advertising: Reimbursement for your advertising efforts. You can be reimbursed up to 25 percent of costs incurred by placing an ad in a publication with a circulation of 10,000 or more.

- eBay keyword ads: Free banner ads up to $200 per quarter
- Value center that offers special values from other companies
- Healthcare solutions for the PowerSellers and their employees
- Invitations to eBay events (i.e., VIP admission to eBay Live and eBay University)

- **PowerSeller Community**

  - Monthly PowerSeller email

  - Quarterly printed *PowerUp!* newsletter

  - PowerSeller-of-the-month success story

  - Exclusive PowerSeller discussion board

- **PowerSeller Recognition**

  - Logo merchandise for you and your customers

  - Logo business templates for customer communications

  - Use of icon next to user ID

  - Use of logo in your item listings and About Me pages

PowerSeller Support

If you sell for a living, timing can be everything. This is another reason why PowerSeller status is a good thing. eBay offers a special system of support for its PowerSellers, as it wants to keep the best sellers active and happy on the web site. Keeping PowerSellers content means more listings, and thus means better business (and profits) for eBay, too.

The PowerSeller Support team usually provides faster and more personalized service to meet a seller's needs and get you back to selling quicker. They accomplish this by categorizing your inquiry to the support staff. PowerSellers receive priority general email support 24 hours a day, 7 days a week, while most trust and safety questions (feedback removal, listing violations, ended-listing concerns, trust and safety issues, billing or just general questions) typically are answered within 36 hours.

part 4

Extra Innings

chapter 10

Trading Safely

The Internet is kind of like America's old Wild West. It's a new land, with all sorts of folks hurrying to join the land rush, trying to stake their claim to a spot in the newest, best part of the open frontier. Opportunity calls and just like the real Wild West, good ol' honest folks are encountering their share of "bad guys" in the computer world.

Today's thieves and culprits don't wear bandanas to hide their faces, and they don't point a gun in their victims' faces and threaten to harm them. That's because they don't need to. All they have to do, actually, while hiding out behind a computer monitor in *who-knows-where*, is send you an email that appears as real as the day is long, but is nothing more than an attempt to steal from you. To take your money. To take your identity. To rob you of your trust.

However, both eBay and PayPal have some built-in safety features to help ward off these cheaters and criminals and scammers. Still, no matter how hard everyone might try, we can't catch all the criminals all the time. That is why it's crucially important for everyone to become aware of, and learn to use some of the well-developed help and safety tools offered by both eBay and PayPal. Even just remembering that they are there to help you just might save you a really bad headache one day, not to mention a huge handful of your hard-earned cash. There also are eBay chat rooms and online support venues to help answer your questions, allow you to deal with trading problems, or just help you find a fellow eBayer's shoulder to lean on during a time of need.

It's 100 percent guaranteed that someone will attempt to spoof you at one time or another by sending you a fake email that might seem genuinely authentic. But I'll alert you to ways to spot the cheaters and hackers before you take a wrong turn and find yourself going down a street that wasn't where you meant to go. Finding and getting rid of the culprits are in eBay's best interests, too—for eBay to succeed, its buyers and sellers must feel safe and successful. So it's no surprise that they have a full-time force of crime fighters who investigate these wrongdoers.

If you manage to learn the safe ways of the eBay trading experience, you'll be better off for it. Remember to keep learning and growing and developing good habits; doing so will help improve your success as a member of the eBay community and save your sanity at the same time. If you click the link to the eBay security center (see Figure 10.1), that also will direct you to several areas that

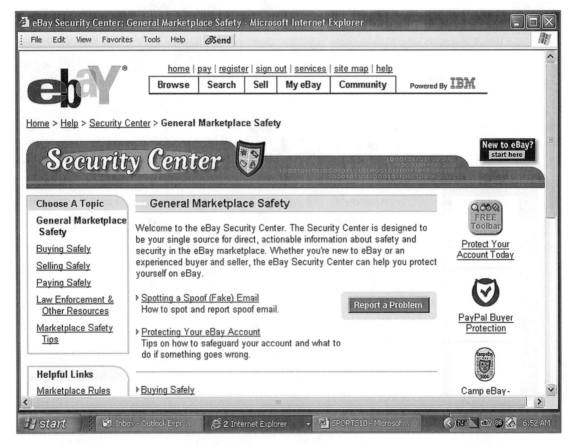

Figure 10.1

The eBay security center provides links to areas that can help answer any trading concerns you might have.

can help answer your queries. There you'll find tips on spotting and reporting spoof email, ways to safeguard your account, what to do if something goes awry, tips on buying, selling, and paying safely, and help from government and law-enforcement sources.

Customer Support

eBay wants your trading experience to be as satisfying and safe as possible, and that means making sure that you get the help you need, when you need it. Clicking the Help link at the top of any eBay page is probably the best way to quickly find the answers to your questions; see Figure 10.2. When you do, you'll be directed to the eBay help center, where you can search or browse through the help topics to find the information you need. To save time later on, it's not a bad idea to bookmark or print out and save the information you find.

If you still need help, click the Contact Us link on the left-hand side of any help page. This will take you to a special form where you can send an email to eBay. Depending on the nature of your question or problem, it usually takes between 24 and 72 hours to receive a response from customer support through email. In some cases, the Live Help button will appear on prominent eBay pages, such as the home page and Sell Your Item form. Clicking that button will connect you to a private online chat room, where you can ask an eBay representative your question. This sometimes is the fastest way to resolve problems.

eBay's help system also can provide quick answers to most of your questions. If you haven't found the information you are searching for, you can email eBay's customer support with the details of your question or issue from the link at the bottom of most help pages. To get the fastest response possible, you should select the help topic that is most closely related to your question.

Follow these steps:

- **Search help:** Type in keywords related to the information you are seeking in the search box at the top of all help pages, then click the Search Help button. You will get a list of related help pages.

- **Use help topics:** Navigate through areas of information to find the information relevant to you.

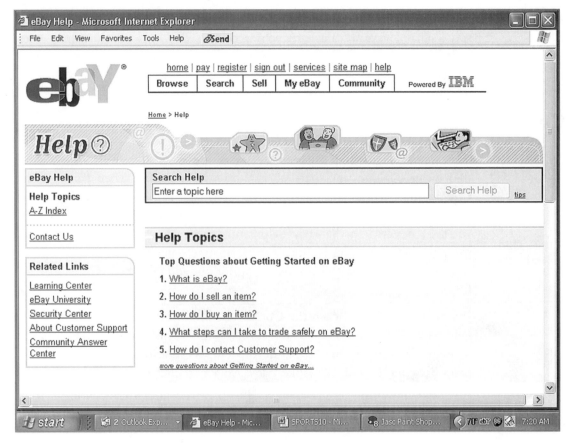

Figure 10.2

Looking for help? Click the Help link at the top of any eBay page. You'll get further directions from there.

- **Use the alphabetical A-to-Z index:** Just click the letter of the alphabet related to what you're looking for.

Don't Get Spoofed

Spoof emails can be a major problem for unsuspecting Internet users. Claiming to be sent by well-known companies, these emails ask consumers to reply with personal information, such as their credit card number, Social Security number, or account password.

These deceptive emails are called spoof emails because they fake the appearance of a popular web site or company in an attempt to commit identity theft. Also known as hoax or phisher emails, this practice is occurring more and more frequently throughout the online world. What you learn here can help you not only on eBay, but wherever you do business online.

They may look real, but there usually are telltale signs (such as misspellings and threats) that help you spot spoof emails. eBay will never ask you for sensitive information in an email. They already have it on file! (See Figure 10.3.)

A common characteristic of a spoof email—one of which is shown in Figure 10.4—is an altered From field. This field can be manipulated easily, so it is not

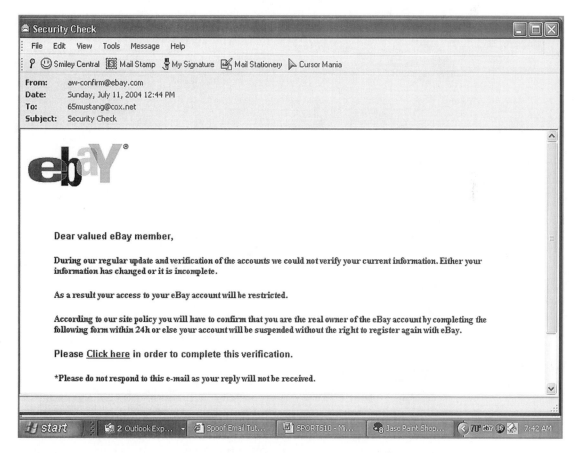

Figure 10.3

Spoof emails may look authentic, but there are telltale signs that raise a red flag.

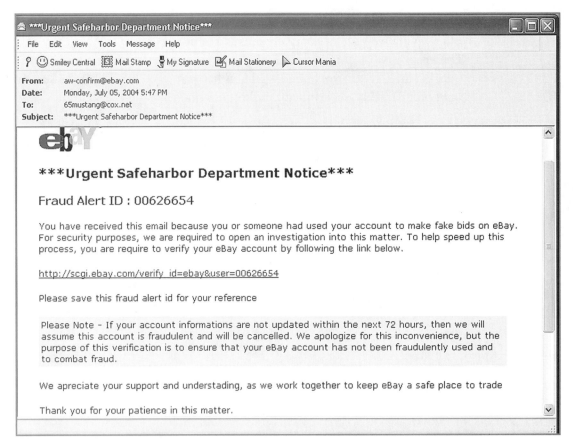

Figure 10.4

Spoof emails are designed to make you worry that you will lose your eBay trading privileges if you don't do what is asked of you. Anything that says "Fraud Alert" is an easy tipoff that you are being spoofed.

a reliable indicator of the true origin of the communication. While there is no single way to recognize whether you have received a spoof email—the senders are especially deceptive—there are a few signs that indicate the email may not be legitimate. A few warning signs to keep in mind:

■ **Sender's email address.** Spoof email may include a forged email address in the From line. Some may actually be real email addresses that have been forged. (For example, From: billing@ebay.com; From: eBayAcct-Maintenance@eBay.com; From: support@ebay.com.) Don't let this fool you.

- **Greeting.** Many Spoof emails will begin with a general greeting such as "Welcome eBay User." The folks at eBay know who you are because of your registration information!

- **Urgency.** The spoofer may claim that eBay is updating its files or accounts. Think about it: It is highly unlikely that eBay will lose your account information.

- **Account status threat.** Most spoof emailers try to deceive you with the threat that your account is in jeopardy and that you will not be able to buy or sell on eBay if you do not update your account immediately. Don't fall for this prank.

- **Links in an email.** While many emails may have links in them, always remember that these links can be forged, too.

- **Request for personal information.** If you are asked to enter sensitive personal information, such as a user ID, password, or bank account number, by clicking a link or completing a form within the email, this is an extremely clear indication you are being spoofed! eBay and PayPal already have this information in their databases from when you signed up to use either or both. Never click a link within an email that you receive if you are unsure of its origin, particularly if it asks you for personal financial information. If you do provide that information, you are looking for big trouble.

There is a bit of good news about spoof emails. By learning how to be cautious and spot them, you can protect your personal financial information. How? By ignoring spoof email altogether. You should never provide contact, sign-in, or other sensitive personal information in an email. It's also a good idea to download the eBay toolbar with Account Guard, which will indicate when you are on an eBay or PayPal site and alerts you to when you are on a potentially fraudulent site.

You can also report the spoofers to eBay. Follow these simple steps:

1. Forward the message to spoof@ebay.com.

   Don't alter the subject line or forward the message as an attachment. Doing so prevents eBay from investigating it further.

2. Once you have forwarded the email, delete it from your email account.

The best advice possible is to be very cautious of email messages that ask you to submit information such as your credit card number or email password. eBay will never ask you for sensitive personal information such as passwords, bank account or credit card numbers, personal identification numbers (PINs), or Social Security numbers in an email itself.

If you ever need to provide information to eBay, please follow these steps:

1. Open a new Web browser.

2. Go to www.ebay.com.

3. Click the Site map link located at the top of the page to access the eBay page you need.

Remember, these tips on avoiding spoof emails apply to PayPal and pretty much any online business endeavor, as well as to your trading experience on eBay. These safety practices should be followed when working with your bank account, ISP account, and virtually any other online account you hold.

Some other tips on keeping safe from hackers:

- **Scan for viruses frequently.** Scan your computer for viruses and make sure your virus software, operating system, and browser patches are up to date.

- **Be vigilant.** It is the best line of defense. You should periodically check your account status to see if there is any suspicious activity.

- **Change your password frequently.** If you think your account security may have been breached, change your account password immediately. Learn how to change your password.

- **Make your password unique.** To prevent someone accessing multiple accounts, it is effective to have different passwords for each account. Also, a good password will include a combination of letters and numbers. This makes it more difficult for people to guess the password.

- **Contact your bank and credit card company.** If you think you entered your personal financial information into a spoof site, contact your bank and credit card company immediately.

Reporting Theft

eBay fully understands that your account security is key to ensuring a positive trading experience. Along those lines, eBay has developed the following steps if you suspect an unauthorized party has gained access to or has attempted to access your eBay account.

- Check with family members and others who may use your account to verify that they did not make any changes. After you have done so, try to sign in to your account. If you are able to sign in, follow the steps in the remaining bullets to secure your account; if you cannot sign in, contact eBay for more assistance.

- Change the password on your email account. Make sure your password is alphanumeric and different than your eBay account password. Ensuring that your email account is secure can help prevent any unauthorized account changes in the future.

- Request a new password. After entering your user ID on this page, you will be prompted to answer at least one of a number of questions related to your account. Once you have answered at least one of the questions provided, an email will be sent with instructions to allow you to complete your password change.

- If you are still unable to change your password, review your eBay contact information carefully to verify that the email address on your account is correct. Also check the spam-filtering settings on your email account to see if the filter is preventing receipt of email from eBay.

- Change the secret question and answer on your eBay account. If you don't have a secret question, make sure to create one for your account.

- Verify that your personal contact information registered on your eBay account is correct. Update any information that is incorrect.

- Search for any active bids or listings that you did not authorize. If you find any unauthorized active bids or listings, you can retract the bids and end the listings. If there are unauthorized fees charged to your selling account, you should contact eBay to request a credit. (To ask for credit, refer to Chapter 8, "Closing the Deal," and follow the same steps as described in "Dealing with Nonpayment.")

Community Help Boards

On eBay's community help boards, eBay members and staff moderators answer questions and try to help you solve problems. Choose a help board and then browse through the topics. Click a discussion topic and you'll see every message in that topic, including these things:

- User ID of the member who posted the message
- That user's feedback rating
- Date and time the message was posted
- A link to the member's listings

To post a message within a discussion, follow these steps:

1. Sign in to eBay.
2. To add a new topic for discussion, click the Add Discussion button at the bottom of any page of topics. Then enter a topic subject and description and click the Add Discussion button.
3. Click the Post Message button at the bottom of any page of messages.
4. Enter your message in the box and click the Post My Message button.

There are also specific chat rooms for people who want to talk just about sports or trading cards. To get to this area, click on the Help tab, and then on the Community Answer Center tab on the left-hand side of the page. That will bring you to another page (see Figure 10.5) that provides links to all the Question and Answer boards, as well as the Discussion boards and Chat centers. By clicking on the Chat tab, you will be directed to an area that includes chat rooms for sports and trading cards. Here, you can ask for help from other eBay users, and perhaps even offer help to other collectors who might have questions that you can help answer. Remember, eBay is a community, and you shouldn't hesitate to reach out for help, or to offer some.

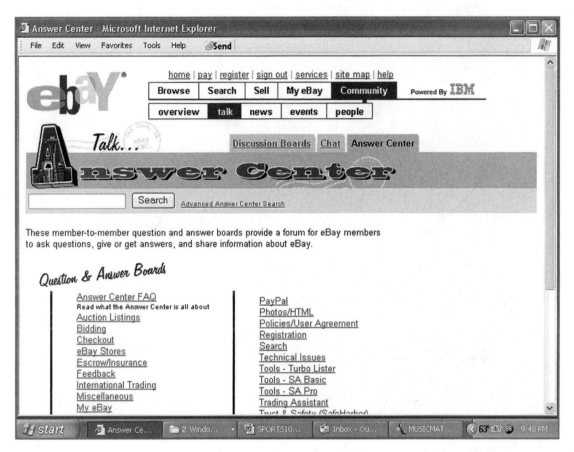

Figure 10.5

Chat rooms and discussion boards are great avenues to find answers to questions you might have about sports collectibles.

chapter 11

Back to the Future

Once you've bought or sold an item on eBay, that's when the real magic begins. The thrill and relative ease of the auction world can generate an infectious enthusiasm; you'll likely want to do more auctions and as quickly as possible. That can bring on a healthy addiction and generate hopes and dreams of exciting career changes, an improved lifestyle, and increased incomes—all so completely opposite of their predecessors, which very possibly have become routinely boring in your life. The dot-com era may have mostly shriveled up and died, but it did help give birth to many home-based businesses that still thrive today.

Why did some home businesses thrive, while others collapsed? Because along with those same hopes and dreams, the businesses that continue to live long and prosper established reasonable and reachable goals for themselves.

It's a well-known fact that a majority of new restaurants have to close their doors after only a short run. Why? Most times, these eating establishments' existence was doomed by a lack of foresight and planning. The restaurant's owners might have ordered exactly the right tablecloths and they might have ordered exactly the right napkins and menus, but they might not have considered that there are a half-dozen other similar eating places on the same street within a short drive of each other. Or maybe their menu prices were too high to compete with the fast-food place on the other corner. Maybe the overhead costs—including wages, supplies, utilities, and the like—were just so much more than they had anticipated, they found it impossible to compete in the marketplace. And after a brief, perhaps even exciting, run, they were forced to turn out the lights, board up the windows, and sell off everything at below cost just to avoid bankruptcy.

It's not uncommon in today's economy, and it's no different than any business wholly or even partially based on income from eBay. There is no getting around doing competent research, devising a solid business plan, and then implementing it—and then reevaluating as you go along, studying trends and changing as the marketplace dictates. A serious approach is required if you plan to go *mano a mano* with the other pros out there who already have secured a steady foothold in the eBay market.

Remember, the established sellers already have several built-in advantages over you. They already have a built-in clientele (auction bidders who have previously purchased from them), and they already have a line of resources (vendors and other dealers who supply products to resell on eBay). Since it undoubtedly has taken a significant amount of time to establish these business contacts, most of the successful sellers aren't going to give you free advice or business contacts out of the goodness of their hearts. You can't blame them, either. Do you think the folks at Toyota want to give their business secrets out to the guys who run General Motors? No way!

Selling full-time on eBay can be fun, but it definitely is not easy. If it were, everybody would be doing it. But with the proper planning and knowledge, it can be accomplished. And once you get started, there are several ways to move forward and make yourself stand out among the rest of the field.

Customer Service

With the huge number of sellers out there on eBay, this concern should be number 1 for you at all times if you hope to find success. If your customers are not satisfied with your level of service, I can guarantee you they won't come back to browse through your auctions later on.

The other area where customer service will pay off for you is through feedback. If you have average or poor feedback from buyers, this definitely will scare off any customers who are deciding whether to try their luck in one of your auctions. Negative feedback from an angry, unsatisfied customer is the kiss of death when it comes to selling on eBay.

Quality customer service also requires prompt and courteous answers to email from buyers. What might sound like a stupid question from a potential customer very well could be an attempt to "sound you out" to see how you treat other people. And if somebody's willing to spend lots of money on one of your sales, you can be sure he will want you to treat him nicely and provide timely replies to any concerns he might have.

Speed Is of the Essence

Another way to set yourself apart from other eBayers is speed. If you're the buyer, the faster you pay for an item, the better feedback you usually will receive on a transaction. And the faster you ship an item to your winning bidder, the better feedback you will obtain as a seller. This is all about customer satisfaction.

The tried-and-true method of deciding how to conduct yourself on eBay is this: Put yourself in the other person's shoes. If you were a seller, wouldn't you want your buyer to pay for his auction as soon as possible, removing all doubts as to whether he will pay at all? And if you were the buyer, wouldn't your trust in a seller skyrocket if you received your purchase so rapidly that it surprised you?

Keep in mind, however, that speed can kill, too. If you handle a transaction too quickly and send the wrong payment amount or the wrong item to your buyer, the odds go up that you will receive negative or neutral feedback from your trading partner. Be quick—but be accurate, too.

Truth in Advertising

One of the easiest ways to kill off your eBay business is to mislead a buyer. If you describe your item as Gem Mint in the auction, it had better be just that or you are looking for trouble. If you say shipping will cost $10 and you charge

$11, be prepared for some angry emails from your customer. A lousy dollar might not seem like much to you, but that amount might have been the reason a buyer chose your auction over somebody else's. Once you've lost a buyer's trust, it's nearly impossible to get it back.

If you change the terms of your auction on the fly, then you're just looking for a headache. Be truthful when you advertise your product and follow through to the letter to please your customer.

Avoid Communication Breakdowns

After an auction is over, be sure to get in touch as soon as possible with your buyer or seller. If you ignore emails about eBay auctions, your trading partner is guaranteed to get antsy. This may seem like a little thing, but a quick, friendly reply to a billing invoice will put you in good stead with a seller, who usually will provide top-notch feedback for your transaction. It also puts the seller's mind at ease that he has communicated with you and that you have all the information you need to complete the deal.

It also doesn't hurt to make a habit out of sending follow-up emails. If you're a buyer and you're pleased with your product and service, remember to leave some good feedback—and perhaps email your seller to tell him you have received your item and that it was a good buying experience.

If you are a seller and your customer has promptly paid for an auction, it doesn't hurt to send an email letting him know his shipment is on its way. You can also:

- Alert customers to any special auctions you might have coming up
- Offer a future shipping discount
- Let customers know about your off-eBay web site

This is just good business and it doesn't take much effort.

Inventory Control

This is a lesson that some eBayers never learn: Once you get started selling, it's inevitable that you will receive inquiries from buyers looking for products other than what you might have up for auction. Even if your buyer has purchased a Derek Jeter bobble head doll, that doesn't mean he's only looking for Derek Jeter products. He might be a devoted Yankees fan or he might collect bobble head dolls.

If you don't know what you have in stock, you may not be able to answer a buyer's question right away. And if it takes you more than a few minutes to answer, remember there are plenty of other sellers out there on eBay who probably sell pretty much the same thing you have to offer. A potential sale to the buyer who had emailed you earlier can easily be lost to another seller if you don't answer his query quickly enough.

A Photo Is Worth . . . Lots!

If a buyer can't see a good photo of the item you are selling, it is bound to sell for less than another seller's similar item, no matter how well you describe it in your auction. A picture is worth a thousand words, right?

A scanner works well for many folks, particularly if the item you are selling is flat, such as a trading card. In fact, a scanner works better than a digital camera for these items because of the lighting and picture quality. Digital scanners can provide a sharper image and more detail than a photograph. Scanners also seem to be going down in price at the same rate their quality level is going up.

If you sell baseballs, jerseys, or framed photos, then a camera definitely would work much better for you. You can pick up a terrific digital camera these days at an affordable price, and it is a tax write-off if you use it for business. It's a piece of equipment, just like your computer or printer. Some things to keep in mind as you shop for a digital camera:

■ **Resolution:** Most experts agree this is the most important determining factor when you purchase a digital camera. The higher pixel count offered, the higher the price of the camera, too.

■ **Manageability:** How easy is a camera to use? Does it feel comfortable in your hands? Is it easily plugged into your computer to download the photos you have just taken? It is simple to understand or do you need to take a night class to figure out how to use it?

■ **Focus:** A camera that offers zoom capability will really come in handy. You don't want to have to be three inches from your subject when you snap the picture. Make sure it has a quality built-in flash as well.

Develop a Brand Name

Once you get started, you want to keep your business going. Along those lines, it's a good idea to set up your own web site, if you haven't already, to advertise your name on the Internet. A web site gives you and your business additional credibility. You can advertise your web site on your About Me page on eBay. This just might be enough to sway a new customer your way if he is having trouble deciding between you and the eBay masses.

Another good way of spreading your good name is to invest a few dollars in some promotional products. Get some professionally printed business cards to hand out at shows, to drop into your package before it is sent off to the winning bidder, or to introduce yourself to potential distributors. You can also print your business name, email address, and phone number on pencils, pens, refrigerator magnets, and even t-shirts. If you remember a product you've previously seen advertised, you're probably more apt to buy it in the grocery store over Brand X.

Do It Right

And finally:

■ You want to offer quality products.

■ You want to offer quality customer service.

■ You want to attract quality buyers.

So don't take shortcuts.

Once you get your business up and off the ground, why go looking for trouble? Remember to keep your mind on quality. Don't stray from the path.

Think about all the national hamburger chains out there. They might add a chicken sandwich or a Caesar salad to the menu, but the good places remember to keep serving quality hamburgers, since this is what put them on the map in the first place. If you add quiche and soup and ice cream to the menu, and your burgers begin to taste like microwaved soybean patties, then you've defeated the purpose and probably lost a lot of customers in the process. When you find what works for you, keep doing it and doing it right.

Additional Resources

If you're about to say, "Hey, he didn't cover this in the book," you'll probably get no argument from me. It's virtually impossible to cover each and every facet of the buying and selling process within a single publication. And with eBay updating, changing, adding, and deleting new features almost every day, it's not unreasonable to expect any book to become outdated. Even good ones, such as this!

For that reason, the following appendix of references hopefully will help point you in the right direction, should you have a question not answered within. These references also are great sources to help you grow your knowledge of sports collectibles as well as the auction process.

Books

***The Official eBay Bible* by Jim Griffith.** Since this was written by one of the first eBay customer support representatives, you know it is loaded with lots of informative tidbits. Written in manual format to help you out with most every facet of eBay. If you're going to make eBay a way of life, this is must reading.

***2004 Baseball Card Price Guide,* 18th Edition.** From the price guide editors of *Sports Collectors Digest.* With more than 20 billion cards sold in 2003 alone, this book offers collectors a practical guide to the marketplace. This guide includes information on some 300,000 baseball cards with information about regular issues, inserts, parallels, and rare variations. Many set listings include photos of cards from that year to facilitate identification. This is a helpful tool that also offers a tutorial on common hobby terms and authentication.

Tuff Stuff 2004 Standard Catalog of Football Cards, **7th Edition.** From the price guide editors of *Tuff Stuff* magazine. Somewhere within these 600 pages you should be able to find information on the football cards in your collection. This guide was put together by Krause Publications, the official collectibles partner of the National Football League. It offers complete coverage of nearly every known football card since 1894, and includes offerings from the NFL, Canadian Football League, and United States Football League, as well as college, food, and regional issues. Keeps you informed so you won't get kicked around by other traders in the know.

Tuff Stuff 2003 Standard Catalog of Basketball Cards, **6th Edition.** Also from the price guide editors of *Tuff Stuff* magazine. Everything you ever wanted to know about collecting basketball cards is probably located somewhere within these 384 pages, which cover prices and listings from 1948 to the present. With many monthly price-guide magazines choosing not to include pricing information about some older or less-popular sets, this book allows you to check on cards from the NBA, WNBA, and CBA, as well as the more oddball offerings from high schools, colleges, and Olympics.

Standard Catalog of Sports Memorabilia, **3rd Edition, edited by Bert Lehman.** This book offers 624 pages jam-packed with pricing information for items ranging from vintage autographs of former sports stars to the latest bobbing head dolls. You'll also find pricing and checklists for autographs, equipment, figures, plates, publications, programs, magazines, books, medallions, press pins and badges, ticket stubs, schedules, pennants, and cereal boxes. You name it, it's probably in here. Be sure to check it out.

Antique Golf Collectibles, **3rd Edition, by Chuck Furjanic.** No, collecting golf memorabilia didn't start with the arrival of Tiger Woods on the professional tour. But a lot of the current memorabilia on the market deals with this long-hitting duffer, and indeed his arrival helped spark a renewed interest in golf cards, memorabilia, and autographs. Furjanic is a golf collector himself, and his book deals with autographs, antique clubs and balls, signature golf balls, books, artwork, ceramics, and trophies. Manufacturer and product histories make this an enjoyable read, as well as a must-have price guide.

Web Sites

AuctionBytes at http://www.auctionbytes.com. A terrific source for news from the online auction industry. Ina and David Steiner launched AuctionBytes in 1999, and their voices have been heard. They publish two free email newsletters and the AuctionBytes Web site, which provides resources for auction buyers and sellers, including statistical information and discussion forums. All provide excellent content that deals with eBay, online trading, and Internet fraud, and they often are quoted by many major news organizations. They even have a Buyers Market where sellers can promote their auctions, web sites, or individual items for sale. Plus, the Steiners have provided annual coverage of eBay Live since eBay first began holding user conventions. Tons of great information on this site.

PSA DNA Authentication Services at www.psadna.com. Here you can find information about getting your autographs authenticated or graded. PSA, a division of publicly held Collectors Universe (NASDAQ:CLCT), was founded in 1991 and now is the largest third-party sports card authentication service. PSA launched PSA/DNA in 1998 and, using state-of-the-art technology, has authenticated such famous items as Mark McGwire's 70th home run baseball and Super Bowl game-used footballs. PSA experts James Spence and Steve Grad have years of experience in collecting and provide professional and unbiased expert opinions on autographs.

Collectors Universe at www.collectors.com. Provides links to several good sources of information that will benefit any collector. Also provides the latest market news.

Global Authentication Inc. at www.gacard.net. Provides interviews and helpful resources about buying cards and how much you should expect to pay for them. Global also is one of the fastest growing authentication services on the sports memorabilia market. Stephen Rocchi (who helped launch PSA) started Global in February 2002 and ever since, they have been grabbing a growing percentage of the graded cards and authenticated autographs market.

Beckett magazines at www.beckett.com. Here you can find information about baseball, basketball, football, hockey, racing . . . pretty much any sports collectible on the market today. Beckett is the leading name in publishing monthly sports collectible magazines. Dr. James Beckett founded the company in 1984; while a professor at Bowling Green in the mid-1970s, Beckett published his first baseball card price guides as free-upon-request pamphlets to, in his own words, "bring order out of the chaos that existed" in the baseball card industry. The official Beckett web site also provides links to several companies and in-house auctions. The company also operates Beckett Grading Services, a leading third-party professional sports card grading service.

Signings Hotline at www.signingshotline.com. Provides information on most every athlete's signing appearance in the United States, along with contact information, pricing (in most cases), and web site links. You can modify your search to include only appearances in your area or for all of the United States. A nifty tool that allows you to link up with most of the major promoters who bring autograph stars into their card shows. This site can help you plan your trip to a show or order autographs from a distant location right on the spot.

Internet Fraud Complaint Center at www.ifccfbi.gov/index.asp. This goal of this site—a partnership between the FBI and the National White Collar Crime Center (NW3C)—is to help prevent Internet fraud. It offers an easy-to-use reporting mechanism that allows traders to inform law authorities of a suspected criminal or civil violation. Here you can also obtain information about complaints related to Internet fraud, fraud patterns, and statistical data of current fraud trends.

Better Business Bureau at www.bbb.org. Have a question about whether the business or charity you might want to deal with is on the up-and-up? This is the place to turn. The Better Business Bureau was founded in 1912 and since then has been helping consumers find trustworthy business partners.

Internet Fraud Watch at www.fraud.org. Includes an 800-number to call for information to help report suspected fraud. You can also get some of the latest news on scams and reported fraud cases.

Identity Theft at www.consumer.gov/idtheft. Run by the Federal Trade Commission, this site allows you to report if somebody has stolen your name, credit card information, Social Security number, or other identifying information. It also offers good advice on avoiding scams.

SquareTrade at www.squaretrade.com. Their goal is to help build trust in transactions and to help improve the online trading experience. SquareTrade aims to help buyers identify trustworthy sellers, as well as help sellers show potential customers that they can be trusted. Many eBay PowerSellers have chosen to include the SquareTrade Seal in their auction listings. SquareTrade's dispute resolution service can also help buyers and sellers work out post-auction problems.

National Association for the Self-Employed at www.nase.org. Founded in 1981 by a group of small-business owners. The NASE provides support, benefits, and consolidated buyer power for small businesses. Hundreds of thousands of entrepreneurs take part in this association, which is the largest nonprofit, nonpartisan group of its kind in the world. Provides help on finance, health insurance, and other important matters confronting the small-business owner.

Publications

Sports Market Report **at www.psacard.com/smrweb.** A monthly buying guide for sports cards and memorabilia. Each issue updates the current market prices for PSA-graded cards, tickets, autographs, game-used bats, and jerseys. Single-issue price is $7 or you can subscribe for a year at $49. If you're into buying and selling sports memorabilia, this can be a valuable $49 investment.

Sports Collectors Digest **at www.collect.com.** This weekly publication, established in 1973, is a must-read if you are into sports collectibles. It covers all aspects of sports collecting, including cards, memorabilia, equipment, figurines, autographs, and graded cards. It also provides interesting stories from collectors, investors, and hobbyists, as well as updated show information.

Tuff Stuff **magazine at www.collect.com.** Established in 1983, offers a comprehensive look at the world of sports collectibles, with information on cards, autographs, and pricing, as well as commentary and opinions from some of the industry's most-recognized names. There are also dealer and product listings, as well as a question-and-answer section.

Index